HOW TO WRITE
a Short Story

D0104351

SPARK PUBLISHING

Written by John Vorwald and Ethan Wolff.

Spark Publishing
A Division of Barnes & Noble
120 Fifth Avenue
New York, NY 10011
www.sparknotes.com

Please submit all comments and questions or report errors to www.sparknotes.com/errors.

Library of Congress Cataloging-in-Publication Data

Vorwald, John.
   [Sparknotes ultimate style]
   How to write a short story / written by John Vorwald and Ethan Wolff.
      p. cm. — (How to write series)
   Previously pulished as: Sparknotes ultimate style : how to write a short story. c2006.
   Includes bibliographical references and index.
   ISBN-13: 978-1-4114-2342-8 (alk. paper)
   1. Short story—Authorship. I. Wolff, Ethan. II. Title.
PN3373.V67 2008
808.3'1—dc22
                         2008019328

Printed and bound in Canada

10   9   8   7   6   5   4   3   2   1

Acknowledgments

Thanks to Margo Orlando for her excellent editing. We also owe a debt of gratitude to Maureen Johnson, whose preliminary work set the tone for this book.

A Note from SparkNotes

F. Scott Fitzgerald once said, "All good writing is swimming under water and holding your breath." Maybe this is how you feel when you face a blank computer screen: desperate, a bit scared, and unable to breathe. Not to worry. Even world-famous essayists, researchers, fiction writers, and poets feel this way every time they sit down to write. Writing isn't easy, and it takes a lot of work to write well. The good news is that writing is a skill you can *learn*.

That's where the How to Write series comes in. We give you everything you need to know about how to write well, from thinking to planning to writing to revising. More important, we give it to you straight, in a concise, stripped-down style that tells you exactly what to do at every stage of the writing process. You won't find any ethereal, "writerly" advice in this book. Instead of "inspiration," we give you all the steps of the writing process in the smarter, better, faster style you've come to rely on from SparkNotes.

SparkNotes How to Write a Short Story is your key to writing great prose. We hope it gives you the confidence to write not only your first word, but also your second and third and fourth . . . Your input makes us better. Let us know what you think at www.sparknotes.com/comments.

Contents

Getting Started

Language is power. It can launch ships, make marriages, and set wars in motion. The act of writing makes language permanent, and words on the page are just as powerful—sometimes even more so—as those spoken out loud. When you write a short story, you use language to create a world. You have control over everything that goes into it, and you're in control of the effect this world has on readers who enter into it. In other words, writing a short story gives you a great deal of power.

A good short story combines the storyline of a spellbinding novel with the intense density of a poem. When you work on such a small scale, you need to maximize the value of each word and phrase—every single thing that goes into a short story must be absolutely vital. The best short stories are full of finely honed, carefully considered pieces—and, if done correctly, a single sentence from a short story can be twisted like a knife into a reader's back. Writing an excellent short story involves more than simply creating a tale with a beginning, middle, and end—but you can master the many elements of the craft with some time, creativity, and practice.

Define *Short Story*

What exactly *is* a short story? *Merriam-Webster's Collegiate Dictionary* defines it as follows:

SHORT STORY short sto•ry *n*

An invented prose narrative shorter than a novel usually dealing
with a few characters and aiming at unity of effect and often
concentrating on the creation of mood rather than plot

"Invented prose narrative" is a long way of saying "fiction."
A "short story" is exactly what it sounds like: it is a story, and
it is short. Pretty much anything longer than a greeting card
inscription will qualify. Some completely legitimate short
stories are only a paragraph or two in length and are called
"flash fiction." It's hard to pull that off and have it amount to
much more than a novelty, but the point is that the category
of "short story" has a lot of flexibility.

Know the Fiction Forms

If you were living in ancient Greece and looking to put pen
to papyrus, you'd pretty much be limited to plays and epic
poems. Over the centuries, narrative form branched out
considerably. Writers began to use central threads, like a
pilgrimage, to tie together unrelated tales. Those short story
collections grew in length and complexity to become novellas, which stretched out further into novels. Today, fiction
writers generally work with the following three forms:

- Novels
- Novellas
- Short stories

Novels   Novels are works of fiction of a substantial length (over 50,000 words is a general benchmark). Novels tend to be both long and complex, so they are usually divided into chapters. Novels are published as books in their own right.

Novellas   Most definitions say that a novella is shorter than a novel but longer than a short story. Generally, a novella fills the gap between the 30,000 words of a long short story and the 50,000 words of a short novel. Novellas can be published on their own as short books, or they can be combined with another novella or a few short stories to make a larger volume. Some examples of novellas include *Heart of Darkness* by Joseph Conrad and *The Strange Case of Dr. Jekyll and Mr. Hyde* by Robert Louis Stevenson.

Short Stories   Short stories are brief works of fiction. Anything under 30,000 words would fall into this category. Short stories are generally not published as books on their own, but you can find them in magazines, online, in anthologies, or grouped together in a book to make a collection.

Choose Your Form

If you want to tell the story of a great warrior's noble thrashing of an arrogant invader, the epic poem may be a valid form for you. If you're more interested in the tale of an office worker going out at lunchtime to buy shoelaces (as Nicholson Baker spent 144 pages describing in *The Mezzanine*), you may find the format of a short novel better suited to the material. If your concept is self-contained, with a limited number of characters, it's begging to become a short story. The difference between a novel and a short story is like the difference between a hit song and a concept album. A concept album will sprawl, examining the various angles that radiate out from its central core. A pop song tends to be tight and harmonious and executed with a certain precision.

Before you start writing, you should consider your material carefully and choose the form that's best for you. Don't use a short story as a fallback—you should choose to write a short story, rather than an epic poem, a novella, or a novel, for a *reason*. One of the main factors in choosing your form may be stamina. Ask yourself if there's enough "meat" on your idea to sustain you through the long process of shepherding a novel or novella to life. If you're not inspired enough to want to dedicate several months to a particular group of characters or a particular time and place, then the short story is the way to go.

Know the Parts

Generally speaking, every short story is made up of the same essentials. You need characters, a setting, and the proverbial beginning, middle, and end. Without certain of these elements, you won't have a story. In general, most short stories have the following parts:

- Title
- Beginning
- Middle
- End

- Setting
- Characters
- Theme

Title   Above everything else stands the title. Often this will provide a glimpse into the story that follows. A title can be any length, from a single word (such as Ann Beattie's "Janus") to a long phrase (such as Flannery O'Conner's "A Good Man Is Hard to Find").

Beginning   Your first sentence, or "lead," may involve more time and effort than any other part of your story. This is your personal introduction to your readers. If you want them to read on to the second sentence, try and hook them with your lead. Beyond the lead, a beginning has a lot of latitude. Some writers advise laying out all your cards from the get-go, with the dilemma visible right from the start. Other stories are better suited to a cryptic start. Sometimes it's best to throw readers right into the howling winds of the hurricane. Whatever tack you take, the beginning is where you turn the key in the ignition and get the vehicle of your story in gear.

Middle   While it's entirely possible to follow certain *Seinfeld* episodes and have a "story about nothing," a lack of content rarely makes a piece any easier to write. You'll probably want to have a plot of some sort, and the middle is the place where it will unfold. The belly of the story is where the conflict will intensify, where your hero or heroine will be tested, and where the elements you've laid out start to breathe. When put together well, the middle can give the end a feeling of inevitability.

End   The resolution of a short story doesn't necessarily tie up every loose end. Sometimes a resolution that makes a story seem even more mysterious makes for a perfect ending. The most important thing is leaving the reader with a sense of *dramatic satisfaction*. The unspoken promises you've made at the beginning and developed in the middle should pay off in the end.

Setting   Stories don't float around disembodied, like restless ghosts. They take place in specific locations, at specific times, during specific eras. Setting is the where and when of a story.

Characters   The characters are the actors who will inhabit the stage created by your setting. The way characters interact —or don't interact—provides much of the richness of a story, even a story focused on only one central character.

Point of View   You have actors and a stage. Now you'll need a director—a narrator with a point of view. Your narrator is the "speaker" of the words in your story. This speaker may have a distinctive voice, a specific agenda, or a unique sense of style. The speaker may be omniscient and as unapproachable as Zeus atop Olympus, or as chatty as your local butcher. The point of view you choose for your story will determine what kind of narrator you have.

Theme   The theme is the underlying "message" of a story, which can be hidden under many layers. Sometimes a theme acts as a moral. In Aesop's fable of the fox and the grapes, the fox that dismisses the distant grapes as being sour anyway is exhibiting the theme "it's easy to hate what we can't have." A theme doesn't always reflect a moral—some stories are created around an idea as simple as "all love is fleeting," or "familiarity breeds contempt." Sometimes you'll know exactly what theme you want to explore when you start writing; other times, you'll figure it out after you've written your first draft.

Read Short Stories

Writers read. According to Stephen King, if you don't have the time to read, then you don't have the time to write. If you want to write short stories, you need to read short stories. The more familiar you are with the art form, the easier it will be to work with. Even if you're planning on breaking every rule in the book, you need to read the book first so you know what exactly it is that you're breaking.

There are thousands of excellent short stories out there—and part of the fun is discovering ones that you love. Here's a list of twenty stellar stories to help you get started (and there are a hundred more we wanted to include):

TITLE	AUTHOR
1. "Cathedral"	Raymond Carver
2. "The Swimmer"	John Cheever
3. "The Lady with the Pet Dog"	Anton Chekhov
4. "The Story of an Hour"	Kate Chopin

TITLE	AUTHOR
5. "The Most Dangerous Game"	Richard Connell
6. "Barn Burning"	William Faulkner
7. "Babylon Revisited"	F. Scott Fitzgerald
8. "The Yellow Wallpaper"	Charlotte Perkins Gilman
9. "The Birthmark"	Nathaniel Hawthorne
10. "Hills Like White Elephants"	Ernest Hemingway
11. "The Lottery"	Shirley Jackson
12. "The Dead"	James Joyce
13. "The Metamorphosis"	Franz Kafka
14. "Odour of Chrysanthemums"	D. H. Lawrence
15. "A Very Old Man with Enormous Wings"	Gabriel Garcia-Marquez
16. "Where Are You Going, Where Have You Been?"	Joyce Carol Oates
17. "The Things They Carried"	Tim O'Brien
18. "A Good Man Is Hard to Find"	Flannery O'Connor
19. "A&P"	John Updike
20. "Why I Live at the P.O."	Eudora Welty

Read Deliberately

Regular readers normally read something just once. Writers will often read something over and over again, sometimes with pencil in hand. They ask themselves the following questions:

- What do I like about this story?
- What do I dislike?
- What parts of this story are most effective?
- Why did the writer choose this character, this model of car, this color for the murderer's cloak?
- What technique can I learn from this writer?

That last question is key. It's been said that a poor writer plagiarizes, while a good writer *appropriates*. Writers don't exactly steal from each other, but they will try to adapt someone else's strengths. Most newly formed bands don't already have their sound nailed down. They start off playing a few covers and gradually develop their own sense of style and taste. Writing is no different. Dozens of twentieth-century literary stars began their careers trying to be Ernest Hemingway. They picked apart his classic short stories, trying to figure out how such wooden dialogue could possibly work so well. Eventually, they discovered that Hemingway's terse style was perfect for Hemingway, but not right for the things they themselves wanted to say.

Learning from the Worst   Excellent, classic short stories aren't the only useful source of learning. Even a clunker can teach you valuable lessons. Look at where a narrative fails to come together, where the protagonist does something jarringly out of character, or where a paragraph repeats the same idea in five only slightly varied phrasings. Picking up on what *not* to do as you read a terrible story is a great way to improve your own technique.

Commit to Starting

A lot of people say they want to write. Unless someone is actually holding a gun to their head and saying "Don't even *think* about it," nothing is stopping them. If you really want to write—*write*. It's that simple. Sometimes the story may come easily, with a ready-made opening sentence and a character that seems to leap off the page. Sometimes you'll have to force yourself to put two words together. Often, the hardest part of writing a short story is just getting around to *starting* it. If you ever want the thrill of tapping out "THE END"—commit now to getting started. Make writing a complete short story a goal, and set aside the time you need to work on it until it's done. You don't have to do it overnight, of course—but don't let your half-finished story disappear into a drawer.

Gather Your Tools

Unlike architects and astronauts, writers don't need a lot of fancy equipment to get a project off the ground. You can get started with simply a notebook and a pen or pencil, or with a computer. A good space to work in is also beneficial. Ideally, your writing space will not be right next to the Xbox, the TV remote, the phone, or the new *Us Weekly*. The most important tool for writing is *time*. Try to dedicate a few hours each week to your writing, and make those hours as regular as possible. Think of that writing time as a personal ritual.

The Writing Journal   One of the most important and effective ways of developing your writing is to keep a writing journal. Unlike a personal diary, where you record your own thoughts, feelings, and experiences, a writing journal is your place to jot down overheard pieces of conversation, to sketch out descriptions of people you see on the street, and to note interesting things you see, smell, and touch as you go about your daily life. Keeping a writing journal is an excellent way to develop your powers of observation—which are vital to a writer. Being attuned to the details of the life around you—a mermaid tattoo on a security guard's arm, a ridiculously inept pickup line—will help you create lively characters and vivid stories. When you want to write a short story, you can open up your writing journal and have a wealth of thoughts, images, observations, and ideas at your fingertips.

A writing journal can also help you develop other skills you'll need as a writer:

- **Sense of humor or drama.** You'll have a better knack for storytelling if you can hone your ability to recognize humor and drama in everyday life.
- **Emotional sensitivity.** To make readers want to get lost in your work, you'll need to be in touch with the humanity of your characters and their problems.
- **A good ear for language.** Nothing throws a reader off as quickly as the clang of a tin ear, especially when it comes to dialogue. If the language sounds false, the story will sound false.

Let Us Show You

There isn't a formula for writing a great short story—and even if you've written hundreds of stories, it's not something you can eventually do in your sleep. Every story is different; every character you create will take on a life of his or her own once you start building a world on the page. In this book, we'll give you all the information you need to put your own story together—what makes a great plot, how to make your characters believable, how to create a rich, detailed setting. Along the way, we'll break down a famous short story called "An Occurrence at Owl Creek Bridge," by the writer Ambrose Bierce, to show you how each lesson plays out in a real piece of writing. At the end of this book, we'll give you the story in its entirety. By that point, we hope you have a complete short story of your own.

Exercises

- Take a favorite short story and make a list of the elements that are revealed in the first few paragraphs. Look for things like the narrator's identity, the time and place that the story is set, and the dilemma being faced by the main character.

- Look around your own desk or–even better–someone else's desk. Jot down the history of five of the objects, making up where they were made, who worked on them, how many others like them still exist, and how they came to rest on that particular desk.

- Take your notebook out to a public place and write brief sketches describing the people you see. At the end of each sketch, write a single sentence that states what that person wants more than anything.

Developing Your Story Idea

Few writers can just sit down and write a story from start to finish, and for a writer, nothing is worse than facing the Great White Abyss (a.k.a. the Blank Page). Before you can type a word, you have to answer a crucial question: *What should I write about?* Sometimes you'll face the abyss with an idea bursting to get out, and you'll have words on the page in no time. Other times, the urge to write might be strong—but you don't yet have an idea. To start figuring out what to write about, stop staring at the page and do some *prewriting*: that is, *developing* your story idea. Don't confuse this for writing your story! This is how you figure out what your shape your story is going to take.

2

   Writing involves both conscious and unconscious influences, and prewriting can help you get in touch with interests, passions, emotions, and opinions that may lead to an idea for your story. Prewriting is actually a misnomer, since much of prewriting is simply deep, focused *thinking*. Prewriting is like brainstorming—getting thoughts, impressions, and random ideas down on the page. So go ahead—let yourself think freely, and story ideas will follow. By putting time and effort into developing your idea, you may find that writing your story comes a little easier.

Look for Ideas in Your Life

To start getting story ideas, ask yourself a few personal questions. Try to get a sense of what you feel passionate about and what people or events from your life might make good characters or scenes for your stories. Thinking specifically about *you* might spark great ideas for your story. Answer these questions in as much detail as possible:

- Who is the person who makes you the most angry? Think of a time in your life when you were angrier than you've ever been before.
- Have you ever been betrayed? Who betrayed you? How did you find out?
- What is your juiciest secret? What would happen if you told someone?
- What do you remember most vividly from the past week? Month? Year? Why does it stand out?
- What is the place you love most in the world? List ten specific things you love about it.
- What is the place you hate most in the world? List ten specific things you hate about it.
- What kind of relationship (mother/daughter, boyfriend/ girlfriend, teacher/student, etc.) is most intriguing to you? Why are you so fascinated by it? What do you think is the hardest part of this relationship, the thing that leads to the most problems?
- Think about books you've read recently or films you've seen. What stands out most in your mind? What connected to you emotionally?

- What impulse is making you write? What do you feel you want to convey by writing a story?

Turning Your Answers into Ideas   Chances are, some parts of your responses will stand out—you'll want to keep thinking about them, or you'll feel drawn to them in some way. Let your ideas marinate in your mind. Start thinking like a writer. Maybe you start thinking about your juiciest secret, and you wonder what would happen if a mother was keeping this secret from her daughter, and they were alone in a beach house for a weekend. Or maybe you think jealousy is the most toxic part of a romantic relationship, and you think you want to write a story about how jealousy leads someone to betray his or her best friend. Suddenly, ideas from your personal life have become ideas for a *story*.

Now you're ready to start enriching your idea with details that will make the story come alive.

Create Conflict

Once you have a germ of an idea for your story, you're ready to figure out what the conflict is. Conflict is the opposition of people or forces against one another. That opposition can take many forms in fiction: it can happen between people, over ideas or feelings, or from natural or manmade circumstances.

Conflict is *essential* to short stories because it will spawn your story's central problem and provide obstacles for your character to overcome before resolving that problem. Conflict activates your characters and creates the tension that engages the reader. When you write a short story, you select and dramatize a defining moment or event in a character's life. That event creates *change*—change in the character, his or her circumstances, and/or his or her life. For that change to occur, your character will have to confront a problem or crisis. Conflict generally falls into two categories: internal and external.

Internal Conflict   Also called *inner conflict*, internal conflict occurs when a character struggles with opposing influences within him- or herself. Internal conflicts produce mental and emotional barriers for your character. Characters that experience internal conflict usually face a difficult question, and the answer to that question often determines how the story is resolved. Here are some examples:

- A man feels guilty because his reckless behavior conflicts with his religious upbringing.
- A woman can't decide whether to tell her best friend that the friend's husband is having an affair.
- A young girl must decide whether to marry a man she doesn't love in order to escape her difficult family life.

External Conflict   External conflict can involve a character who struggles against another character, or a character who struggles against an external force, such as nature, fate, destiny, or even God. External conflict creates tangible obstacles for your character to overcome. Here are some examples:

- A hero with a mission must fight against a villain who tries to keep him from completing that mission.
- An adventurous sailor must fight for survival when a storm traps her at sea for three nights.
- A young boy born into poverty struggles to escape his circumstances.

Choose Your Conflict Type

Internal and external conflicts are not necessarily exclusive. For example, a rock climber might have to scale a steep, treacherous mountain (external conflict). After falling on a previous climb, however, she questions her own abilities and judgment. The character must then not only overcome the mountain's terrain but also the fear and self-doubt in her mind (internal conflict). You don't have to choose one type of conflict over the other. Many great stories utilize both kinds of conflict to heighten the tension. Here are some questions to consider when choosing conflicts for your story:

- What kind of conflict do you want to highlight in the story? Will it be an internal conflict or an external conflict—or both?
- Which conflict is appropriate for your characters' desires and actions?
- Which conflict is appropriate for the setting?
- Does the conflict offer a difficult struggle for your character?

If your story idea is vivid in your mind, you may find that you have easy answers to these questions. If your idea is still sketchy, then thinking carefully about conflict will help you fill out some of the details. This is all part of the process of prewriting, of developing your story idea.

Ask the MDQ

Embedded in every story is a big question that's begging to be answered—the "What happens?" question. Will the hero succeed or will the villain stop him? Will the girl get the guy? Who killed the teacher? This is called the *Major Dramatic Question* (MDQ), and it represents the gap between the story's problem and its resolution.

The MDQ serves as a compass for every story because it points to the story's defining event or climax. Short stories demand precision, and if you know your story's MDQ from the very beginning, you'll write a story with more specific direction and have a better understanding of what needs to happen at the climax. To figure out the MDQ for your story, consider the following questions:

- What, if anything, does my character want?
- What action does he or she take to get what he or she desires?
- What, if anything, keeps my character from getting what he or she wants?
- Who succeeds? Who fails?

Answer the MDQ

As the author of your story, you not only get to ask the MDQ, you get to answer it. Your answer will determine how the story is resolved. Keep in mind that even if your character succeeds in getting what he or she wants, the story's resolution might not necessarily be a happy one. In Nathaniel Hawthorne's story "The Birthmark," for example, a scientist succeeds in removing a birthmark from his wife's otherwise perfect face, only to see the process take her life. He gets his wish but loses something far more valuable. The way you resolve the central conflict or problem in your story will not only determine how the story unfolds but also shape the change in your character and his or her circumstances. It will also affect the theme of your story.

Expand Your Story Idea

You've come up with an idea for your story, and you've thought about conflict and the MDQ. But it's not time to write yet! First, you need to fill in more of your story's details. You may have a specific vision for your story already, or you may just have shadowy characters and a tentative idea of what their conflict is. Either way, considering details carefully and committing them to paper is an important step in developing your story idea. You should make your idea as lively, layered, and detailed as possible before you start writing.

Earlier, you asked yourself questions about *you* to come up with some ideas for your story. Now you need to ask yourself some questions about your *story*, including the characters, conflict, and resolution. Not all of it may make it into the story itself—but some of it will, so make your answers as detailed as possible.

Character

1. Who is my main character?
2. What does my main character look like?
3. How old is he or she?
4. What makes him or her angry? Happy? Sad?
5. What's his or her family like?
6. How does he or she get along with peers? Does he or she have friends?
7. What events in his or her life led him or her to the main event in the story?
8. Who are some of the other characters? How do they relate to the main character?

We'll talk in more detail about creating characters in Chapter 3.

Conflict

1. What does the main character want?
2. How does he or she try to get what he or she wants?
3. How do his or her actions affect the other characters?
4. How do his or her actions affect the setting?

5. What obstacles keep my character from getting what he or she wants?

6. What does the character do to overcome those obstacles?

Resolution

1. Does my character succeed in getting what he or she wants?

2. What, if any, consequences are there for the main character's actions?

3. How does he or she change because of his or her actions?

4. Is the character better or worse off when the central problem is resolved?

Diagram Your Story

Before you start writing your story, consider diagramming it. Creating a diagram can give you a clearer idea of your story's movement—where the character starts, the problems he or she faces, and the resolution. When you eventually do start writing, you won't be writing into an abyss: you'll know where your story is going.

Making a "V" Creating a "V" diagram is an easy and effective way of sketching out the movement of your story. Identify the three most important points in your story's beginning, middle, and end, and write them into a "V" diagram like the one on the next page. As your story takes shape, you may want to fill in additional details, such as the conflict that leads the character to the story's central problem and the obstacles that he or she must overcome before the problem is resolved:

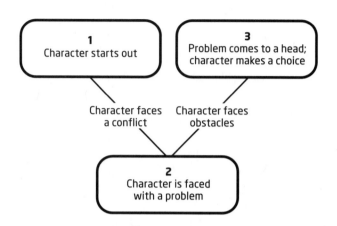

Diagramming in Action   Let's make a "V" diagram for our model story, Ambrose Bierce's "An Occurrence at Owl Creek Bridge."

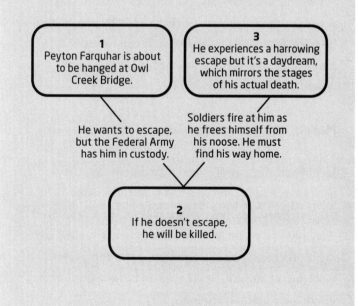

Sum It Up

At this point, you should have enough details about your story to be able to write one clear, concise paragraph that sums it up. This is called a *synopsis*. Briefly introduce your main character and the setting of the story. Then describe the conflict that the character encounters and what actions he or she takes to overcome it. Tell what, if anything, changes in the life of the character when the crisis is resolved.

Now go crazy: try to do all that in one clear, concise sentence. Distilling your story down to its essence will help you get a clear picture of exactly what you're writing.

Summing It Up in Action   Let's see what a synopsis looks like for our model story, "An Occurrence at Owl Creek Bridge":

Peyton Farquhar, a well-to-do Southern planter, is to be hanged by the Federal Army in Civil War–era Alabama. A Federal scout posing as a Confederate soldier tricks him into tampering with Owl Creek Bridge, and the punishment is death. While being hanged, Farquhar escapes his noose and swims away from his captors amid gunfire. The sensations he experiences during his escape mirror the physical effects of asphyxiation. After a harrowing journey, Farquhar returns home. However, as Farquhar sees his wife emerge, we learn that his escape was imagined—a final daydream before dying of a broken neck from hanging.

After writing a story paragraph, it's easier to distill the story into one sentence:

A Southern planter avoids hanging at the hands of the Federal Army, only to realize his harrowing escape was a final daydream before dying of a broken neck.

Exercises

- Reread one of your favorite short stories. Identify the main character, the main conflict or crisis, and how the character resolves it. Sketch a "V" diagram for the story.

- Think of three of your favorite movies. Write down the MDQ for each movie.

- Write a one-paragraph description of your favorite short story. Be sure to include details about the character, the problem or conflict, how it is resolved and how the main character changes at the conclusion of the story.

Characters

Once you've spent some time thinking about and developing your story idea, you'll most likely know what characters you're going to be moving through your fictional world. The question you must answer now is one of the most exciting of the story-writing process: *Who*, exactly, are these characters? When you write a short story, you need to know your characters—every one of them—as deeply as you know your best friend. In a sense, you're like Dr. Frankenstein, creating his monster. Every aspect of your character is yours to create.

A great short story has compelling, *believable* characters who are complex and interesting. There may be just one main character, or there may be a whole crew; but each and every character in your story must take on a life of his or her own. Figuring out the basics, such as name and hair color, isn't enough. You need to think deeply about what makes your characters tick and how they will operate in the world of your story.

3

Know the Types

There are three types of characters that will populate your short story:

- Protagonist
- Antagonist
- Supporting characters

Each type of character plays a different role in your story. Before you create your own characters, you must understand the function of each type.

Protagonist   A *protagonist* is the star of your story. *Pro-* means "for," so your protagonist is working for or toward a goal. The protagonist wants something—something essential. Whatever this *something* is, it's usually very important to your character. This one thing—the object of desire—is critical because it will determine the focus of the story. Your protagonist will almost always be working against an antagonist, which is something or someone who wants to stop the protagonist from getting what he or she wants.

If your antagonist is a person, figuring out who is the protagonist and who or what is the antagonist isn't always as easy as figuring out who's the good guy and who's the bad guy. A protagonist isn't always likable, and a human antagonist can be downright magnetic. Your protagonist may be a murderer who wants more than anything to get away with his crime and leave the country.

Antagonist   *Ant-* means against, so an *antagonist* is a force or a character that works against the protagonist, standing in the way of his or her desires or plans. An antagonist can be anything at all, such as weather, fate, or a personal phobia. If your antagonist is a person, he or she is not simply the "bad guy." If your protagonist is indeed a murderer, the antagonist could be a police detective, trying to catch the murderer and ruin his plans for escape. What's important is that the antagonist, whatever or whoever it is, is working to keep the protagonist from getting what he or she wants.

Supporting Characters   If the main characters dictate the direction of a story, supporting characters help move the story further along that route. *Supporting characters* are complementary characters that propel a story forward by helping to generate or diffuse conflict. Supporting characters can sometimes give added dimension to the protagonist or antagonist. That doesn't mean that supporting characters are always friendly with or even familiar with the main characters; they may hover on the margins of your character's life. If your protagonist is a beat reporter, for example, your supporting character might be one of his sources, a demanding editor, or another journalist. They may not be friends, but their circumstances (and the circumstances of the story) dictate that they work together or that their paths cross.

Define the Desires

When you developed your story idea (see Chapter 2), you decided what the main conflict of your story would be. And if you know your story's conflict, you know your protagonist and antagonist. You may not have fully fleshed-out characters yet, but you have a rough sense of what your protagonist is working for and how or why your antagonist is working against him or her. Now it's time to examine your characters' wants in detail and figure out who your characters (if there's more than one) *are*—what makes them tick, why they're seeking what they're seeking, or why they're fighting what they're fighting.

The *Whys* In developing your story idea, you've already spent some time thinking about what, exactly, your protagonist and antagonist want. But now's the time to go further and figure out those wants in more detail. Ask yourself the basic questions—then keep asking yourself "Why?":

What does your protagonist want?

- Why does he or she want it?
- Why is it so vital to him or her?
- What will success mean for him or her?
- Why hasn't he or she sought it until now?
- Why is this particular moment so important?

If your antagonist is a person, what does he or she want?

- Why does he or she want it?
- Why is it so vital to him or her?
- What will success mean to him or her?
- Why is he or she determined to triumph?
- Why is he or she "against" the protagonist?

Since the protagonist is your main character, it's most important to figure out his or her *whys*. But having at least some understanding of your antagonist, if it is a person, will help make your story richer.

Define the Needs

Your protagonist's desires determine the action of the story. But where do they come from, and what makes them interesting? A woman who works to become wealthy because of greed is much less interesting than a woman who works hard to become wealthy because she needs the approval of her hard-to-please parents. As a writer, you must identify your character's wants, but you must also connect those wants to your character's *needs*.

Needs are deeply entrenched motivators that drive people's behavior. They're different from wants in one vital way: they are often not consciously acknowledged by the character. Your character may know very well that she yearns to become wealthy—but she may not be consciously aware of her deeper motivation, her need for her parents' elusive approval. You as the writer must figure out your character's needs even if your character isn't aware of them.

Psychologist Abraham Maslow identified five basic needs that drive human behavior. You don't have to be a psych student to write a short story—but a basic understanding of these different kinds of needs might help you to better understand where your character's desires come from:

1. Physiological (body) needs
2. Safety needs
3. Social needs
4. Needs for esteem
5. Need for self-actualization

Physiological (Body) Needs   These are the needs for oxygen, food, water, sleep, etc. These things are necessary for survival, so these needs are the strongest and most basic. Body needs can control thoughts and behaviors. When they are not met, they can cause people to feel sickness, pain, and discomfort. Take a look at this example:

> A homeless woman, who must find a way to feed herself everyday, probably spends most of her energy and concentration trying to find food. Even seemingly basic impulses like the need to bathe come a distant second to the need to eat and drink.

Safety Needs   When all body needs are satisfied, the needs for safety become more pronounced. These consist of the needs for physical safety (such as shelter) and personal security. Children often have a more acute sense of safety and personal security than adults. When a person feels a sense of immediate danger, safety needs can eclipse body needs. For example:

> A young child may enjoy playing under the watchful eye of her mother or father. If the mother or father disappears from the setting, however, the child will likely turn his or her attention to locating the parent. The child needs to know that the parent —the shield from danger—is watching again before he or she can continue to play.

Social Needs   These are the needs for love, affection, and belonging. They emerge when the needs for safety and for physiological well-being are fulfilled. People want to be accepted, whether in clubs, work groups, religious groups, family, or gangs. They need to feel loved and accepted by others. Without love and acceptance, people become increasingly susceptible to feelings of loneliness and alienation. Few social needs are as powerful as the need for social acceptance, especially from peers. Consider the following example:

> A high school student who doesn't fit into the dominant culture (the popular crowd) will probably seek out alternatives for social acceptance. Some might gain acceptance by playing sports. Others might form a band, participate in theater, or just find a few like-minded friends who don't fit in with the popular kids either.

Needs for Esteem   These involve the need for both *self*-esteem and the esteem a person gets from gaining the respect of others. People need a stable, high level of self-respect and respect from others. When these needs are not satisfied, a person can experience feelings or inferiority and worthlessness. When the needs for esteem are overindulged, a person can have a bloated sense of self or snobbishness. For example:

> A girl who plays high school soccer might meet her social needs by becoming an accepted part of the team. As she emerges as the team's best player, she also meets her esteem needs. She takes pride in knowing she is among the best at her sport, and as a result of her playing prowess, she is held in high regard by her teammates and the coaching staff.

Need for Self-Actualization   The need for self-actualization is the need a person feels to do what he or she feels he or she was born to do. A person who has not achieved self-actualization may feel on edge, tense, lacking something, or restless. This need is often most visible when it is not being met. Take a look at this example:

> Consider a man with a natural aptitude for language and words. His need for a sense of financial security led him to pursue a career in finance when he graduated from college. While he is competent at his job, he often feels restless, as though his work somehow ignores his true strengths. He makes good money, but he can't shake the feeling that something is missing.

Connect Wants and Needs

Once you have a sense of what your character *needs*, you should figure out how those needs connect to what your character wants in your story. Try to write a few sentences describing this connection. Consider the following questions; we provide an example for each regarding a character named Jean to show how each question might operate in a short story:

- **Which needs are satisfied in his or her life?** Jean comes from a middle-class household; her body and safety needs are met.
- **Which needs are not satisfied?** New to her high school, Jean has not yet developed a group of friends. As a result, she doesn't feel accepted. Her social needs are not met.

- **What occupies his or her thoughts most of the time?**
  Jean often thinks about these questions: How do I make
  friends here? What do I have to do to belong?
- **How do his or her needs inform his or her wants and
  desires?** Jean's unmet social needs dictate her desire
  to ingratiate herself to her new classmates, to become
  accepted by a group at the school.

The goal is to anchor your characters' wants and desires—
and ultimately their actions—in deep-rooted needs. If your
characters are motivated by needs, rather than by, say, divine
goodness or gratuitous malice, their desires and actions will
be more believable and engaging.

Assemble Your Cast

Your story may have only a protagonist and an antagonist, or
it may have a larger cast of supporting characters. How do
you decide how many characters you actually need? A good
way to begin is to think about what your story demands. That
is, what does the story *need* to move forward? A good rule of
thumb is that every character in your story must propel the
plot forward in some way—every character must be necessary. Think of each character as having a job to do to help
tell the story.

Defining Roles   Let's say your protagonist thinks her
house is haunted by a ghost. She wants to make sure she's
not crazy, and she also wants to know if there really is a
ghost. As the writer, you can help her address this problem

by creating another character. Instead of doing the investigation all on her own, she invites a friend over to help her. This new character has a *job* in the story—to help confirm or contradict the protagonist's suspicions.

Let's say the protagonist invites *two* friends over. One friend agrees there is a ghost inside. The other believes there is a perfectly logical explanation for the moving furniture and strange, white gusts of wind. Each of these new characters has a distinct disposition. Furthermore, they are *opposing* dispositions, and these dispositions reflect the protagonist's inner conflict: is there a ghost, or isn't there? Each character has a role that helps to bring about the resolution of the story.

As you assemble your characters, try to define their role in the story. Ask yourself the following questions:

- What is this character's job?
- Does the character help generate or resolve the conflict? How?
- Does this character help your protagonist resolve the story's central problem? How?
- Does this character help the antagonist provide obstacles for your protagonist to overcome? What obstacles?

Making the Cut   Since short stories give you limited room to operate, you can't let characters in if they don't have a purpose. No character gets to just hang out, even for laughs. To make the cut, a character should fulfill at least one of the following functions:

- Help generate or diffuse conflict
- Provide obstacles or help the protagonist remove them
- Add dimension (through contrast or similarity) to the other characters

If a character doesn't meet one of these criteria, he or she doesn't make the cut. Even if a character seems important at first, you may have to ax him or her later. You can always reintroduce this character in another story, another day.

Show, Don't Tell

Good writers aspire to *show* rather than *tell* about their characters. Showing is almost always more interesting and effective than telling. Take a look at these two examples, in which we try to describe a character named Claudia:

Claudia was a very jealous woman.

As soon as Paul was asleep, Claudia emptied his backpack, flipped through the contents of his wallet, and checked the call-log on his cell phone.

The second example is much more compelling because we're *showing* that Claudia is jealous, rather than simply saying so. You can reveal characters skillfully by showing readers what they do, what they say, what they look like, and how they live. In other words, you can reveal characters in a three different ways:

- Action
- Dialogue
- Description (of both appearance and environment)

Action   Characters are revealed by what they *do* and the *decisions they make* in a story. Portraying your character's actions is one of the most effective ways to reveal his or her nature. These actions can be extravagant, such as a teenage boy camping out on the front lawn of the house where his crush lives in order to prove his affection to her. They can also be small gestures, such as a woman brushing an eyelash from her young daughter's cheek while she's sleeping. Both big actions and small gestures can create a vivid portrait of your character.

Actions can even be things the character *does not* do: for example, a man may always neglect to kiss his wife before he leaves for work in the morning. Sometimes the overlooked actions and forgotten gestures are the most poignant.

Dialogue   Characters are revealed both by *what* they say and *how* they say it. Dialogue is one of your most useful tools as a writer. Dialogue reveals a character by conveying how the character relates to other characters. Is the character witty and outgoing, or reserved and quietly intelligent? Is she comfortable talking to others, or does she seem to prefer to be alone? Who has the power in the relationship between the characters who are speaking to each other? Well-written dialogue can answer these kinds of questions and help paint a fuller picture of the character's interpersonal skills and style.

Dialogue in Action   P. G. Wodehouse uses dialogue effectively to reveal his characters and establish the dynamics between them. Look at this passage from his short story "Jeeves Takes Charge," in which young master Bertie Wooster interacts with his butler, Jeeves:

> "Oh, Jeeves," I said; "about that check suit."
>
> "Yes, sir?"
>
> "Is it really a frost?"
>
> "A trifle too bizarre, sir, in my opinion."
>
> "But lots of fellows have asked me who my tailor is."
>
> "Doubtless in order to avoid him, sir."
>
> "He's supposed to be one of the best men in London."
>
> "I am saying nothing against his moral character, sir."
>
> I hesitated a bit. I had a feeling that I was passing into this chappie's clutches, and that if I gave in now I should become just like poor old Aubrey Fothergill, unable to call my soul my own. On the other hand, this was obviously a cove of rare intelligence, and it would be a comfort in a lot of ways to have him doing the thinking for me. I made up my mind.
>
> "All right, Jeeves," I said. "You know! Give the bally thing away to somebody!"
>
> He looked down at me like a father gazing tenderly at the wayward child.
>
> "Thank you, sir. I gave it to the under-gardener last night. A little more tea, sir?"

We can infer a lot about the two characters from this short conversation. We first notice that Bertie asks Jeeves to comment on his "check suit," which Jeeves thinks is "too bizarre." When Bertie retorts that others have asked for the suit tailor's name, Jeeves responds, "Doubtless in order to avoid him, sir." Right from the start, we know that Bertie values Jeeves's opinion. We can also see that Jeeves is funny and perhaps the smarter one of the two. Bertie confirms this for us in his narration; he says that the butler has a "rare intelligence" and worries that he may be passing into the "chappie's clutches." Who has the power here? Bertie tries to reestablish rank, ordering Jeeves to "Give the bally thing [the suit] away to somebody!" But Jeeves is one step ahead: "I gave it to the under-gardener last night," he says.

From this small bit of dialogue, we know that Jeeves is not only more intelligent than Bertie but that he has power over his master. Within a few lines, Wodehouse has clearly revealed the character of a witty and intelligent servant who seems to have his master wrapped around his finger. And he didn't have to tell us anything explicitly—he showed us his characters through dialogue.

Description   A character's appearance can be one of the first indicators of personality. While it would be easy to describe a character from head to toe, this can be tedious for readers. When describing your characters, choose the aspects of their appearance that tell something about who they are. Maybe the protagonist's suits are always pressed because he's trying to impress his boss. Maybe he's a student who always looks like he just rolled out of bed, or maybe an otherwise clean-cut guy has a tattoo on his arm. Think about what these things say about your character's personality.

Likewise, your character's environment can speak volumes. Is the house messy or neat? Are there shoeboxes stacked in the closet, each with a label describing what's inside, or are there chaotic piles of things on the closet floor? Are the walls painted white, or red? Is your protagonist's purse stuffed full or nearly empty? Revealing key details about your character's environment can serve as a kind of shorthand for what he or she is like on a deeper level.

Description in Action   Virginia Woolf begins her story "The Duchess and the Jeweller" with a description of the main character's house:

> Oliver Bacon lived at the top of a house overlooking the Green Park. He had a flat; chairs jutted out at the right angles—chairs covered in hide. Sofas filled the bays of the windows—sofas covered in tapestry. The windows, the three long windows, had the proper allowance of discreet net and figured satin. The mahogany sideboard bulged discreetly with the right brandies, whiskeys, and liqueurs. And from the middle window he looked down upon the glossy roofs of fashionable cars packed in the narrow straits of Piccadilly.

We learn quite a lot about Oliver through this description of his environment. First, we have a name: Oliver Bacon. Think about bacon: it's a fatty, tasty meat. It implies fullness, but it's not fancy. Bacon suggests common origins. It's a basic English name. We know that Oliver lives on the top floor, right in the center of London. He looks *down* on things. We know that he has very nice, very appropriate, probably expensive furniture.

Notice that the words *discreet* and *right* appear twice. There is "discreet net" on the windows, and the sideboard "bulged discreetly" with a selection of the "right brandies, whiskeys, and liqueurs." (The other "right" describes the angles of the chairs.) This is no accident. Everything suggests that Oliver is correct and careful about what he shows. The net on the windows means we can't really see what's inside of Oliver's home. Also, it's not really possible to "bulge discreetly." We know that Oliver wants for nothing—he's got all the right stuff—but he does just enough to make sure his things aren't completely on display. Yet the fact that everything he has is "right" means that he's definitely conscious of his possessions.

From this description, we get someone rich, physically contented, and conscious of the rules, someone with a common name who is cautious about showing off his belongings. Perhaps he grew up poor? Perhaps he has to be careful of something? Later in the story, we find out that this is all true. Oliver grew up poor but is now the most successful jeweler in London. As a jeweler, he must always take care of his jewels; it's obvious that he owns lots of them, but he must keep them hidden away in order to protect his wealth. Those seven seemingly house-focused sentences turn out to be full of information about the character.

Balance Your Characters

No characters are *all* good or *all* bad. One-dimensional characters are not only unrealistic; they're not very interesting to read about. If conflict creates a compelling story, complex people make more engaging characters. That complexity comes from a character's strengths *and* weaknesses.

This is especially important when creating protagonists and antagonists. Everyone loves a compelling bad guy, and heroes are more human if they must work to overcome their flaws. Even good-natured protagonists will have flaws and inner conflicts. And ill-mannered antagonists may have understandable intentions. Exploring the good and the bad within all your main characters will make your characters more believable. In real people, good and bad qualities are often intertwined. A person's strengths often inform his or her weaknesses.

Balancing Characters in Action   Creating balanced characters means exploring many different sides of their personality and figuring out how their strengths and weaknesses are intertwined. Take a look at two complex characters that we've created:

PROTAGONIST: Our protagonist is a brilliant forensic anthropologist. Having earned her doctorate from Yale, she is extremely bright, discerning, and entirely committed to her work. Those qualities have made her a professional success, but they have also nurtured her biggest weakness: long hours in the lab have led her to ignore her social life. As a result, she lacks social grace. She feels awkward around people, and she is often perceived as aloof and even arrogant. She has few close friends or intimate relationships, which makes her interaction with other characters in the story more challenging.

ANTAGONIST: Our antagonist is a former dictator of a small Central American country who now lives in Europe. He worked his way through the ranks of his county's army as a soldier and finally came to power as a general through a military coup in the 1980s. Although his regime was cooperative with the United States, it often acted brutally against its own people. Though he was seen as a gregarious leader, political opponents and anyone who voiced public opposition to his leadership often disappeared mysteriously, never to be seen again. After a series of mass graves is discovered, the International Criminal Court has begun an investigation into the dictator for the murders of thousands of his own citizens. When a brilliant forensic psychologist from the United States is hired to examine the bodies and gather possible evidence for an international trial, the dictator begins a secret campaign from abroad to intimidate her and undermine her work.

In these examples, the characters' strengths and weaknesses have a natural and understandable relationship to one another. By creating good and bad qualities that inform and complement one another, you'll draw more realistic characters.

Make a Character Chart

A character chart can help you nail down aspects of your character that you might not have otherwise considered. It will help you think about specifics—things that might seem unimportant, or even irrelevant to your story. For now, try to think about your character as independent from your story. Try to think about him or her as a real person. When your character is very real to you, some of that realness will come through in the story.

You can write in your answers right on the chart on the next two pages, or on a separate sheet of paper. You can also make copies of the chart so that you can use it again and again.

Using the Chart   Once you've filled out a character chart, how do you *use* it? Many of the characteristics you flesh out in the chart won't make it into your story, but knowing these details can still influence how you present your character on the page. Familiarity with the intimate details of your character will not only deepen your understanding of the character; it can also help you envision how he or she would react in a given situation—and why.

Let's say you fill out a character chart and decide that your protagonist is epileptic—a condition that gives him sudden seizures. He just moved to a new school, and he doesn't want to tell his new classmates about his condition out of embarrassment. How does his secret affect how he interacts with the other students? Maybe he's more nervous than usual. Maybe he isn't as social as he might be otherwise. If he likes a girl, does he hesitate to talk to her, or does he ask her out? Does he worry about having a seizure in front of her? Does he ask her out anyway? You may never reveal the character's condition in the story, but knowing his secret helps you to better understand how he might behave.

Character Chart

Character name

Gender

Age

Profession

Where he/she lives

Appearance

Eye color

Glasses or contacts

Weight

Height

Type of body/build

Skin tone

Shape of face

Notable features

Hair color

Type of hair (straight, curly, balding, etc.)

Hairstyle

Is he or she in good health?

      If not, why not?

Physical disabilities

Favorites

Color

Music

Movie

Food

Clothing

Prized possession

Background & Family

Hometown

Relationship with mother

Relationship with father

Siblings

    How many?

    Describe relationship

Place in the birth order

Extended family?

    Describe relationship

Personality

Greatest fear

    Why?

The worst thing that could happen

Most at ease when

Most uncomfortable when

Most embarrassing past failure

Darkest secret

    Does anyone know?

    If yes, did character tell them?

    If no, how did they find out?

Greatest strength

Greatest weakness

Biggest vulnerability

Biggest accomplishment

Biggest regret

Interpersonal Skills

How does character relate to others?

How is he or she perceived by others?

What do others like most about character?

What do others like least about character?

Forget Reality

You might be tempted to model a character on someone you know—or even on yourself. Writers do this all the time, but it's harder than you think, and there are some serious pitfalls to be aware of. Before you populate your story with your parents and your high school classmates, there are a few things you should know.

First, you may think that since your character is based on a real person, he or she will automatically be realistic in the story. Actually, the opposite is true. Because you know this person so well (especially if you base the character on yourself), you may neglect to provide your reader with the kinds of basic details that can reveal so much of a character in a story. Or, you may be tempted to show this real person in all his or her idiosyncratic glory—only to wind up with a haphazard character who doesn't make much sense on the page. Sometimes, reality just doesn't translate into fiction.

When you try to keep your character true to the real person, your story will suffer because you won't feel free to be creative. Remember: every character must have a vital role in your story. Even if you start off basing a character on a real person, let yourself deviate from or embellish reality to serve your story's progress. Change things. Combine several different people into one character. Try to forget what you know about the real person and let your character react as your *character*, not as the person. If your changes and embellishments render the character unrecognizable from your initial inspiration, remember that this is fiction. It's *meant* to be made up.

The Real-Life Fallout   If you decide to base a character on a real person, keep in mind that this person may very well be flattered or complimented but may just as easily get upset with how you portrayed him or her. You shouldn't write your story with the constant worry about what others will think of it. But if you *do* show your story to the person one of your characters *very strongly resembles*, be prepared for the fallout.

Love All Your Characters

All of your characters are your creations. Think of them as family: you don't always *like* them, but you must *love* them. All characters have a function in the story, but not all of them will be—or should be—likable. Some of them will be deeply flawed and even occasionally malicious. Resist the urge to hate or become indifferent to your most unsympathetic characters. That can lead to oversimplified villains and heroes, instead of complex human characters. If you write a story centering around a character you consider ideal, remember that no one is perfect. Acknowledge and *use* the character's flaws. If you're tempted to create an antagonist that seems purely evil, play Luke to his Darth Vader: you have to believe there's some goodness in there somewhere. Find his strengths and balance them against his weaknesses.

Character in Action   Take a look at how Ambrose Bierce creates character in this passage near the beginning of "An Occurrence at Owl Creek Bridge":

> The man who was engaged in being hanged was apparently about thirty-five years of age. He was a civilian, if one might judge from his habit, which was that of a planter. His features were good—a straight nose, firm mouth, broad forehead, from which his long, dark hair was combed straight back, falling behind his ears to the collar of his well-fitting frock coat. He wore a mustache and pointed beard, but no whiskers; his eyes were large and dark gray, and had a kindly expression which one would hardly have expected in one whose neck was in the hemp. Evidently this was no vulgar assassin. The liberal military code makes provision for hanging many kinds of persons, and gentlemen are not excluded.

Bierce withholds a very basic piece of information about his main character: his name. Bierce does this intentionally. Think about what a name can add to a character: it personalizes the character, makes him individual, and gives him a specific identity. By not naming his character right away, Bierce keeps the character's personal identity a mystery, choosing instead to reveal the character through more observable features, such as his age. The description seems more objective and therefore credible, as though it were written by an impartial reporter.

Bierce then describes the man's appearance—his "habit," face, and build. We learn that he has "good" features. Bierce uses repetition to make a point: the man has a "straight nose" and combs his hair "straight back." He also has a "firm mouth" and "broad forehead," and he wears a "well-fitted frock coat." He may be about to be hanged, but Bierce's description suggests that this is an earnest, straightforward man who takes care of himself. Before we can rush to judgment about his predicament, we also learn that his eyes have a "kindly expression." Bierce tells us that he is no "vulgar assassin" and implies that he is a gentleman.

Without commenting on whether the man is actually guilty, Bierce lets us know that there is something about the character that appears to be good. The character also seems to lack the treachery we would normally associate with a common criminal. Has he been mistried? Is he the wrong man? What has he done to be hanged? With just one paragraph of description, Bierce has provided a sketch of his protagonist and managed to imply that the protagonist's personality and circumstances don't quite match.

Exercises

- Write a paragraph that describes how your protagonist spends the week before the story starts. Now do the same for your antagonist, if your antagonist is a person.

- Write down four things that your protagonist and antagonist would most like to change about themselves. Explain why. (Skip the antagonist if it is not a person.)

- Write a one-paragraph self-description in the voice of each of your supporting characters.

Point of View

The who, what, where, and why of your story are important, but just as important is the how: that is, how you tell your story. How you tell your story will affect your reader's experience just as much as your characters, setting, and plot. When you start thinking about how you want to tell your story, what you're really thinking about is point of view: the perspective from which the story is told. Someone needs to tell your story, and even if that someone never appears in the story, his or her view will color everything.

Point of view serves as the camera lens for readers. Their "view" is limited to whatever you, the writer, offer—readers can't see anything beyond what you put on the page. Sometimes the lens will be a wide-angle, providing lots of details about a wide range of characters, time periods, and subjects; and sometimes the lens will be a telephoto, focusing closely on one specific person, moment, or event. Sometimes the view will be well-focused and sometimes it will be unreliable, or blurry. The point of view you choose is how you reveal your story to the world.

4

Know the Types

Every story has a point of view. There are three different types, called "persons": first-person point of view, second-person point of view, and third-person point of view. Each works in a very different way.

First-Person   First-person point of view is a narrator speaking directly to the reader. This narrator is usually, but not always, a participant in the story. This is the "I" point of view, and you'll use first-person pronouns: *I, me, we, our, mine, my.*

Second-Person   Second-person point of view is the "you" point of view. The writer tells the story as if the reader is living it, such as: "You go to the corner store and see your former lover." Some readers are turned off by the second-person voice because it makes them feel like they're being bossed around by the writer.

Third-Person   Third-person point of view is the writer speaking. There are no limits for this point of view, and it has the potential go anywhere, including into the minds of all the characters. You'll use third-person pronouns: *he, she, they, it, them, theirs, his, hers.*

Consider First-Person

Using the first-person creates a sense of immediacy in your story. A first-person narrator is in the middle of all the action, reporting on what is happening in the present or recounting what happened in the past. A first-person narrator is usually a character in your story. With first-person point of view, you're limited by the fact that the narrator can't tell you what he or she doesn't know. First-person narrators can't go into the heads of other characters, and they can't describe scenes or events that they themselves aren't in.

Sometimes first-person narrators are forthcoming about the fact that they're telling a story. They may even explain why they're telling it: for example, maybe they want you to believe they're not crazy, just misunderstood. Other narrators just jabber on, oblivious to the reader, and it becomes the reader's task to figure out what's important and what can be believed. The approach you choose will depend on how much distance you want to keep between your narrator's mind and your audience.

Voice   When you use the first-person point of view, you "speak" as a character in the story and give that character a voice. A narrator can be amped, throwin' down slang a mile a minute, or as stiff as a starched collar, exhibiting a virulent preference for multisyllablic expressional formats, or any of the zillion alternative voices in between. A third-person narrator also has a "voice," but the voice it reflects is generally the writer's.

First-Person in Action   When you use first-person point of view, you can convey your narrator's personality instantly. Take a look at the opening lines of Charlotte Perkins Gilman's "The Yellow Wallpaper":

> It is very seldom that mere ordinary people like John and myself secure ancestral halls for the summer.
>
> A colonial mansion, a hereditary estate, I would say a haunted house, and reach the height of romantic felicity—but that would be asking too much of fate!

> Still I will proudly declare that there is something queer about it.
>
> Else, why should it be let so cheaply? And why have stood so long unattended?
>
> John laughs at me, of course, but one expects that in marriage.

One of the most noticeable things about this section is that it's made up of a series of short declarations. There's barely time for full sentences here, much less full paragraphs. The narrator seems to have run up to us, out of breath, hair tumbling loose, dying to tell her story. These short sentences set up a brisk tempo.

The narrator is also giving us some facts. We learn that the narrator and her husband are regular people, meaning they probably aren't sitting on piles of excess cash. Yet they've still managed to afford the rent on a mansion—strange, unless there's something terribly wrong with the mansion. The narrator is building a little suspense while simultaneously conveying her anxiety, which shows in the way her thoughts are flying every which way. First-person point of view pulls us right into the narrator's jittery state of mind. The narrator also tells us that her husband doesn't take her thoughts very seriously. This is personal stuff—thoughts that could be embarrassing—that paint the narrator's marriage in a pretty poor light. The narrator isn't going to hide behind rose-colored glasses. She's going to put her trust in the readers as she lays her situation on the line.

Determine Reliability

The *reliability* of your narrator is his or her *trustworthiness*.
First-person narrators can provide trustworthy background
information and observations, or they can be warped, with
abnormal or unusual takes on things. When you decide to
use first-person point of view, you have to choose whether to
make your narrator *reliable* or *unreliable*.

How do you choose? You may have to experiment.
Sometimes an unreliable narrator is too untrustworthy for
readers to want to spend much time with. Sometimes a reliable narrator is too boring to make a story truly compelling.
See what works best for your particular character and story.

Reliable Narrators   You can trust that what reliable narrators tell you is true. When they describe a scene or another
character, they may filter it through their own biases, but for
the most part what they say is going to match reality. For example, when a reliable narrator says that her boss was pleased
with the ideas for the new ad campaign, the reader can be
confident that the boss wasn't actually trying to communicate
that it was a travesty of a presentation and that everybody's
getting fired in the morning. You should make your narrator
reliable if you want to give your readers a trustworthy guide
through your story.

Reliable Narrator in Action   Take a look at the respectable narrator John H. Watson, M.D., at the beginning of the
Sherlock Holmes story "The Adventure of Wisteria Lodge"
by Sir Arthur Conan Doyle:

I find it recorded in my notebook that it was a bleak and windy day towards the end of March in the year 1892. Holmes had received a telegram while we sat at our lunch, and he had scribbled a reply. He made no remark, but the matter remained in his thoughts, for he stood in front of the fire afterwards with a thoughtful face, smoking his pipe, and casting an occasional glance at the message. Suddenly he turned upon me with a mischievous twinkle in his eyes.

Dr. Watson, the narrator, seems extremely objective. He is telling us the facts with the cool observational skill of a trained medical professional. What Watson sees is exactly what we get—Sherlock Holmes drives most of the action in these tales. With such close observation of Sherlock, it can be easy to forget that the narrative is in first-person. It almost seems like Watson is the voice of the author.

Though Watson seems trustworthy, he isn't perfect. Sometimes he makes a less-than-brilliant observation, and he tends to put Holmes's achievements in a heroic light. Still, we don't feel as though we're stepping through a minefield of untruths and misconceptions when we're following Watson. He can be *relied* upon to accurately recount what's going on.

Unreliable Narrators   Unreliable narrators may be drunk, high, or insane—or they may simply have an ulterior motive to telling the story. They may have an ax to grind or may be so angry that they can't think straight. For a reader, an unreliable narrator's misunderstandings can be hilarious, poignant, suspenseful, or confusing. It's often a good idea to let your readers know immediately that your narrator is unreliable so that they know that the point of view is slanted and should be taken with a grain of salt. You should make your narrator unreliable if you want his or her secrets or agenda to have an effect on the story being told.

Unreliable Narrator in Action   Take a look at the narrator of Edgar Allen Poe's story "The Tell-Tale Heart":

> No doubt I now grew very pale—but I talked more fluently, and with a heightened voice. Yet the sound increased—and what could I do? It was a low, dull, quick sound—much such a sound as a watch makes when enveloped in cotton. I gasped for breath—and yet the officers heard it not. I talked more quickly—more vehemently; but the noise steadily increased. Why would they not be gone? I paced the floor to and fro with heavy strides, as if excited to fury by the observation of the men—but the noise steadily increased. Oh, God; what could I do? I foamed—I raved—I swore! I swung the chair upon which I had been sitting, and grated it upon the boards, but the noise arose over all and continually increased. It grew louder—louder—louder! And still the men chatted pleasantly, and smiled. Was it possible they heard not? Almighty God!—no, no! They heard!—they suspected—they knew!—they were making a mockery of my horror!—this I thought, and this I think. But anything was better than this agony! Anything was more tolerable than this derision! I could bear those hypocritical smiles no longer! I felt that I must scream or die!—and now—again!—hark! louder! louder! louder!
>
> "Villains!" I shrieked, "dissemble no more! I admit the deed!—tear up the planks!—here, here!—it is the beating of his hideous heart!"

This narrator doesn't sound like the kind of person we'd like to draw as our first-year college roommate. Poe's choppy fragments show off the deranged state of his character's mind. The narrator tells us that the thumping sound filled the room while the officers ignored it with "hypocritical smiles." The reader has so little faith in the reliability of the narrator, however, that it's easy to draw alternative conclusions. The sound is all in the narrator's head, a delusion caused by the guilt he feels over the murder. The cops aren't hypocrites; they're genuinely clueless about what the narrator is hiding, at least until he completely loses it and admits the crime. The sound of his own heart beating has driven him over the edge.

By using an unreliable narrator, Poe gives us a more immediate portrait of what insanity really feels like. And by forcing us to separate reality from delusion, we become more engaged in the story.

Consider Second-Person

When you use second-person point of view, you treat the reader as a character in your story. Second-person point of view is the point of view used least often by writers. It's tricky to use because it can make a story seem like a "choose your own adventure," where you are actually a character in the story and the writer is telling you what to do: "You go into the haunted castle . . ." "You wonder whether you should open the unlocked door of the cupboard. . . ." Readers can be turned off when they spend a few pages being told what to do. Take a look at this example:

> You walk into the forest. You spend hours gathering firewood, then set about building a fire. You open your backpack and take out a can of stew. You realize it's going to be a very long night.

Second-person can be aggressive, since you're basically ordering your readers around. It's not impossible to do effectively, and you should consider giving it a try. But be aware that it's often not a good way to appeal to readers.

Second-Person in Action   Take a look at how Nathaniel Hawthorne uses second-person point of view in this paragraph from his story "The Haunted Mind":

> You sink down and muffle your head in the clothes, shivering all the while, but less from bodily chill, than the bare idea of a polar atmosphere. It is too cold even for the thoughts to venture abroad. You speculate on the luxury of wearing out a whole existence in bed, like an oyster in its shell, content with the sluggish ecstasy of inaction, and drowsily conscious of nothing but delicious warmth, such as you now feel again. Ah! that idea has brought a hideous one in its train. You think how the dead are lying in their cold shrouds and narrow coffins, through the drear winter of the grave, and cannot persuade your fancy that they neither shrink nor shiver, when the snow is drifting over their little hillocks, and the bitter blast howls against the door of the tomb. That gloomy thought will collect a gloomy multitude, and throw its complexion over your wakeful hour.

Hawthorne wrote in the 1800s, but what he describes still rings true today—on a cold morning, cocooned in covers, the last thing we want is to get out of bed. And sometimes lying half-asleep leads the mind to wander in unpleasant directions. Hawthorne makes this scene immediate by using second-person point of view. We as readers can't escape the specters of disappointment and shame that the narrator goes on to describe. They seem to be happening to us.

At the same time, Hawthorne keeps the concepts abstract enough so that we don't feel like we're under the heel of a dictatorial narrator. Hawthorne doesn't specify the disappointments and shames, so it's easier for us to distance ourselves from the really morbid impulses. In this case, the second-person point of view is an effective way of allowing readers to fill in their own specters.

Consider Third-Person

Third-person point of view gives you the ability to get close to your characters without actually having your narrator be a character in the story. One advantage of third-person is that it feels objective. As the writer of your story, you have authority, and this authority really comes through in third-person narration. And if you want to inject a little gravity into a piece, it can be easier to do from third-person.

One of the problems with the third-person is that you lose some of the urgency and intimacy that first-person conveys. There's a layer of insulation between the character and the reader. But you can overcome this limitation by really getting deep into your characters' minds and making those characters vivid and many-layered. There are two different types of third-person point of view: *omniscient* and *limited.*

Third-Person Omniscient *Omniscient* means *all-knowing*. When you write from the third-person omniscient point of view, you can see everything and hear everything. In a way, using third-person omniscient point of view is like playing God. Omniscient narrators have the power to read the mind of anyone in the story. They can fly across the boundaries of space and time. The problem with third-person omniscient point of view is that with the compressed action of a short story, it may be *too* powerful. There often isn't room to do justice to every character. When it comes to short stories, many writers choose instead to limit the point of view.

Third-Person Omniscient in Action Take a look at the opening of O. Henry's famous short story "The Gift of the Magi":

> One dollar and eighty-seven cents. That was all. And sixty cents of it was in pennies. Pennies saved one and two at a time by bulldozing the grocer and the vegetable man and the butcher until one's cheeks burned with the silent imputation of parsimony that such close dealing implied. Three times Della counted it. One dollar and eighty-seven cents. And the next day would be Christmas.
>
> There was clearly nothing to do but flop down on the shabby little couch and howl. So Della did it. Which instigates the moral reflection that life is made up of sobs, sniffles, and smiles, with sniffles predominating.
>
> While the mistress of the home is gradually subsiding from the first stage to the second, take a look at the home. A furnished flat at $8 per week. It did not exactly beggar description, but it certainly had that word on the lookout for the mendicancy [begging] squad.

This narrator is *omniscient*. He knows what it felt like for Della to save up the $1.87, and he knows the unhappiness she feels as she recognizes how inadequate a sum it is. But this narration isn't restricted to Della's mind. Once she starts sniffling, the narrator pokes around the apartment. The notes on the décor aren't filtered through Della's own perceptions of her home. (If Della was looking around her own home, she probably wouldn't describe it as a beggar's home.) Instead, a wry, disembodied voice that has a crystal-clear view of the big picture fills us in.

Third-Person Limited   A third-person limited narrator is a fenced-in version of the omniscient narrator—that is, this narrator can see into the mind of only one character. All of the observations will be from that character's perspective. In a short story, where there may not be time and space to explore the inner workings of several characters, the third-person limited narrator can be the best way to put a frame around events. Though you miss out on the total power of the omniscient, you still have plenty of versatility.

You may choose to apply third-person limited point of view to several characters, shifting from one perspective to another over the course of a story. This can be effective, but it's often better for novels, when there is much more room to adequately explore several characters. Multiple perspectives are usually too much for a short story.

Third-Person Limited in Action   Take a look at an
excerpt from the beginning of Anton Chekhov's short story
"The Bishop":

> How stifling, how hot it was! How long the service went on!
> Bishop Pyotr was tired. His breathing was labored and rapid, his
> throat was parched, his shoulders ached with weariness, his legs
> were trembling. And it disturbed him unpleasantly when a religious
> maniac uttered occasional shrieks in the gallery. And then all of a
> sudden, as though in a dream or delirium, it seemed to the bishop
> as though his own mother Marya Timofyevna, whom he had not
> seen for nine years, or some old woman just like his mother, came
> up to him out of the crowd, and, after taking a palm branch from
> him, walked away looking at him all the while good-humouredly
> with a kind, joyful smile until she was lost in the crowd. And for
> some reason tears flowed down his face. There was peace in his
> heart, everything was well, yet he kept gazing fixedly towards
> the left choir, where the prayers were being read, where in the
> dusk of evening you could not recognize anyone, and–wept. Tears
> glistened on his face and on his beard. Here someone close at hand
> was weeping, then someone else farther away, then others and still
> others, and little by little the church was filled with soft weeping.
> And a little later, within five minutes, the nuns' choir was singing; no
> one was weeping and everything was as before.

The impressions of this scene aren't given by a distant author. Bishop Pyotr himself directs the point of view, which is
limited to his observations. When he's bored and restless, the
scene is conveyed in a negative light. As his emotions shift,
the setting shifts as well. The remainder of the story stays

close to the bishop, with the narrative frequently returning to the bishop's thoughts and emotions.

Consider Other Points of View

When you write a short story, you'll usually use either the first-person or third-person point of view. However, there are other points of view you can consider, and experimenting with them may open up new doors for you in your writing.

Stream-of-Consciousness   Stream-of-consciousness writing can appear unedited, as it reflects the thoughts of a character as they come streaming through the mind. It's harder to pull off than it sounds: it's difficult to make the routine babble of thought entertaining enough to keep a reader interested. Stream-of-consciousness reached its height of popularity in the first half of the twentieth century, and it feels a little dated now, but experimenting with it may give you new insights into your characters. These three works employ a stream-of-consciousness style:

- *A Portrait of the Artist as a Young Man* by James Joyce
- "The Snows of Kilimanjaro" by Ernest Hemingway
- *On The Road* by Jack Kerouac

Monologue   Writing in a monologue style means basically giving a speech on paper. You become an actor standing alone in a spotlight, addressing the audience (or a specific group or person, such as an ex-lover) directly. These thoughts tend to be more focused, and therefore more polished, than stream-of-consciousness. A monologue can be tricky to pull off: in getting rid of the other characters, props, and setting, you give up some of the tools that help make writing come alive. These three works employ monologue:

- "The Pit and the Pendulum" by Edgar Allan Poe
- "The Lady's Maid" by Katherine Mansfield
- *The Dying Animal* by Philip Roth

Diary or Journal   When you write in a diary or journal style, you write as though your character is writing directly into his or her notebook. It has the potential to be more intimate than the monologue, which is heard by an audience. However, the diary or journal style potentially suffers from the absence of dramatic tools, just as the monologue does. These three works are structured as diaries or journals:

- *Dracula* by Bram Stoker
- *Bridget Jones's Diary* by Helen Fielding
- *Rites of Passage* by William Golding

Epistolary   *Epistle* means "letter," and the epistolary point of view takes the form of a letter from one person to another, or a correspondence between two parties. It was highly popular in the days before cars and telephones, when people communicated primarily through letters. Don't feel beholden to pen and ink, however: you may consider updating this form by creating a correspondence made up of emails or instant messages. Check out these three works to get a sense of the epistolary style:

- *S.* by John Updike
- *Griffin and Sabine* by Nick Bantock
- "Letters to the Editore" by Donald Barthelme

Point of View in Action   Take a look at the following excerpt from the beginning section of "An Occurrence at Owl Creek Bridge":

> He closed his eyes in order to fix his last thoughts upon his wife and children. The water, touched to gold by the early sun, the brooding mists under the banks at some distance down the stream, the fort, the soldiers, the piece of drift—all had distracted him. And now he became conscious of a new disturbance. Striking through the thought of his dear ones was a sound which he could neither ignore nor understand, a sharp, distinct, metallic percussion like the stroke of a blacksmith's hammer upon the anvil; it had the same ringing quality. He wondered what it was, and whether immeasurably distant or near by—it seemed both. Its recurrence was regular, but as slow as the tolling of a death knell. He awaited each stroke with impatience and—he knew not why—apprehension. The intervals of silence grew progressively longer, the delays became maddening. With their greater infrequency the sounds increased in strength and sharpness. They hurt his ear like the thrust of a knife; he feared he would shriek. What he heard was the ticking of his watch.

Bierce is conveying the feelings of a condemned man standing on the gallows in his final moments. The scene derives its power from the *third-person limited* point of view, which makes the reader no wiser than Farquhar, the main character. Like Farquhar, we wonder what the "sharp, distinct, metallic" sound is, and our wondering increases the tension of the scene. Only at the end of the paragraph does Farquhar realize the sound is actually the ticking of his watch—and we the readers make this discovery right along with him.

If Bierce had taken an omniscient stance, he might have told us at the very beginning of the paragraph that Farquhar's anxiety was being heightened by the ticking of his watch. As Farquhar wondered and worried about the source of the sound, we would already have known what it was. The effect of fearing the seeming "tolling of a death knell" would have been lost.

In fitting with the constraints of third-person limited point of view, Bierce keeps his narration narrowly focused. We don't get the thoughts and sensations of the soldiers charged with executing Farquhar, and we don't get inside the head of Farquhar's wife. Bierce's self-imposed limits help to place us right in the middle of the action, and we feel exactly what Farquhar feels. And although we're in the thick of things, we're not totally swamped by the panic that might consume a first-person narrator. The third-person limited point of view was exactly the right choice for this short story.

Exercises

- Write a scene from the perspective of a first-person narrator. Then write the exact same scene using third-person limited point of view. See what changes occur with the shift in perspective.

- Write a short scene about a misunderstanding between two people. First write it from the one person's point of view, and then write it again using the other person's interpretation of the same events.

- Describe a dinner conversation between a couple where the narrator knows he or she is being cheated on. Then try the same conversation, only this time make the affair obvious to the reader, while the narrator remains clueless.

Beginnings and Endings

In a short story, you don't have much room to connect to your readers, so beginnings and endings are important: you need to hook your readers in and leave them with a strong, lasting impression. Unlike a novel, where you can introduce your characters and story leisurely over several paragraphs, pages, or chapters, in a short story you have to grab your readers immediately. An intriguing first sentence is vital, and a great second sentence doesn't hurt. The more irresistible you make your opening lines, the more likely it is that your readers will keep reading.

If the beginning is your introduction to your readers, the ending is your final send-off—and possibly the thing they'll remember most. There are many ways to end a story, and you may have to approach the ending from a few different angles before you get it right. The ending is where your readers will look for meaning, and it's important not to let them down. How you begin and end your story will depend on the story itself, but there are some things you can learn about both beginnings and endings that will help you become a better writer.

Pull the Trigger

Most short stories have something called an *inciting incident*. This incident is what sets the story in motion. Think of the inciting incident as the "trigger" that's going to "fire the bullet" of your short story. Once you pull the trigger, there is no turning back.

The trigger doesn't have to be a violent incident; it can be as quiet as a guy getting dumped and deciding to change his life, or a woman digging through the attic for a scarf and finding a forgotten photograph. In a short story, the trigger sets up the conflict. Since you don't have any time to waste in a short story, you should get to this incident as soon as possible—within the first few passages.

Finding the Trigger   You've got your setting. You've got your conflict. What you need now is something to get you from one to the other. The trigger is the thing that's going to disrupt the stable environment of your setting. What event is going to throw off the equilibrium? You have lovingly populated the private detective's office with the bronze eagle paperweight, the whiskey in the file cabinet, and the peeling lettering on the door. Description of an office interior does not a short story make, however. You need a dame to walk in, her fingers reeking of gunpowder, dabbing her eyes and announcing that her husband has gone missing. The arrival of the case is the trigger. The problems that arrive in solving the case will be the conflict.

Hook Your Readers

In the very beginning of your story you'll "hook" your readers, with the hopes of reeling them in. It takes some originality to make your story stand out from the rest and get readers engaged. The very first sentence is crucial, and you'll have to figure out what detail or clue to include that will spark your readers' interest and compel them to read on.

Your trigger can work as your hook. If you have a compelling event, like in Franz Kafka's "The Metamorphosis," where the narrator wakes up and discovers himself transformed into a giant bug, you'll grab many readers. Your hook doesn't have to be a trigger, however. It can be an intriguing setting, voice, or a particularly dramatic line of dialogue. One of the most reliable ways of guaranteeing a reader's attention is setting up a dilemma. If it looks impossible to solve, so much the better. The key is to get the hook under the reader's skin, so when you start to tug on your line, the reader can't resist following. Here are the triggers from some famous short stories:

- The trigger of "The Magic Barrel" by Bernard Malamud is the engagement of a matchmaker by a young rabbinical student.
- "You Were Perfectly Fine" by Dorothy Parker is triggered by a young man waking up with a cataclysmic hangover and trying to piece together the strands of the previous night.
- John Updike's "A & P" has as its trigger the entrance of three girls in swimsuits into a grocery store.
- In "Everything That Rises Must Converge," by Flannery O'Connor, the trigger comes when the main character starts accompanying his mother to a weight-loss class.
- Raymond Carver's "Are These Actual Miles?" is triggered by the need to sell a car.

- In Kate Chopin's "A Respectable Woman," the trigger is the arrival of an old college friend at a couple's plantation.
- The trigger of "The Killers" by Ernest Hemingway is the entrance of two out-of-town strangers into a lunch room.
- In "A Rose for Emily," by William Faulkner, the trigger is the death of Miss Emily Grierson.
- The arrival of Scrooge's cheerful nephew acts as the trigger for Charles Dickens's "A Christmas Carol."
- The beginning of the lottery itself functions as the trigger for "The Lottery" by Shirley Jackson.

Put Something at Stake

Once you introduce the trigger at the beginning of your story, you have to give readers a reason to care about your character and what he or she is facing. This is how you get them to keep on reading. Answer this question: "What's at stake for my character?" Conflict is essential, but the consequences of that conflict are even more important.

For example, say you have a couple getting married. If they've just met in Vegas and they're getting hitched on a drunken whim, with a prenuptial agreement signed in the lobby, we won't be very invested in how long the marriage lasts. If, however, we learn that the groom secretly needs a Green Card so he can stay in the United States because if he's deported back to his home country he'll be tortured and executed for once speaking out against the dictator there, well, that's a whole different story. Now we're curious about how he'll have to act around his new bride, how he'll have to bend over backward to hide his secret and to keep her happy, no matter how bad a fit for each other they turn out to be.

Try to make the stakes clear at the beginning. This will build the tension, which is what makes readers turn pages.

Find the Starting Place

There are infinite possibilities for how you can begin your story—the difficulty of writing a first sentence or first paragraph is enough to paralyze a lot of writers. Perhaps the most important question you need to ask yourself is this: Where in my story should I begin? A story doesn't need to begin with the trigger. You may begin with some setup, leading slowly into the trigger and action. (Though in a short story, you can't spend too much time leading in.) You may begin in the middle of the action, just after the trigger has been pulled. Or you can start with the conclusion and then work your way back, showing how the trigger led to the action, which led to the ending the reader has already seen. Where in your story you choose to begin will determine where you place your trigger, which will set your action in motion.

There are three possible strategies for handling your story's starting place:

- Setup
- *In medias res*
- Flash forward

Setup   Many short stories open with a background sketch or background information, called *exposition*. This can cover anything from the setting to the main character to the inciting incident. A "sketch" is really what it has to be—in a short story there isn't the time or space to indulge in wandering descriptions. A good setup provides a stage where the action can play out. This is the way to go if you want to ease your reader into the story.

Exposition can be valuable, but be careful not to overdo it. Try to give readers a little credit—often it takes only a couple of clues for them to start catching on. Paragraphs upon paragraphs of back story can be more wearying than informative. And a short story's compressed format makes "cutting to the chase" all the more essential.

Setup Beginning in Action   Leo Tolstoy is famous for writing very long novels, but he was also adept at the short story format. Take a look at how he begins his story "God Sees the Truth, But Waits":

> In the town of Vladimir lived a young merchant named Ivan Dmitrich Aksionov. He had two shops and a house of his own.
>
> Aksionov was a handsome, fair-haired, curly-headed fellow, full of fun, and very fond of singing. When quite a young man he had been given to drink, and was riotous when he had had too much; but after he married he gave up drinking, except now and then.

> One summer Aksionov was going to the Nizhny Fair, and as he
> bade good-bye to his family, his wife said to him, "Ivan Dmitrich, do
> not start to-day; I have had a bad dream about you."

Right from the first sentence we learn our main character's name, location, and occupation. In sentence two we find out how successful he is, and by sentence three we've been given the brushstrokes for his looks and personality. Tolstoy hasn't gotten to the trigger and the action yet. He wants to flesh out his main character first, so we have some grounding before things start happening.

Note that although Tolstoy gives us background to work with, he isn't starting off the story with Ivan's first day of kindergarten or his relationship with his parents. He's only got enough space to rough out the essential facts, and then it's on to the crux. Tolstoy picks the fateful day of the journey to the fair as the best starting place for Ivan's tale. And we're immediately curious about his wife's dream. Somehow we know that Ivan should be heeding the premonition, though of course there's no way he will.

In Medias Res   *In medias res* is Latin for "in the middle of things," and that's exactly where you'll drop your reader if you choose this technique. Background and explanatory information are put aside for the moment, and sometimes readers will have to work a bit to figure out what's going on or who's saying what. Jump-starting the action without delay is a very popular way of beginning a short story.

In Medias Res Beginning in Action Take a look at how H. G. Wells uses an *in medias res* beginning in his story "The Cone":

> The night was hot and overcast, the sky red, rimmed with the lingering sunset of mid summer. They sat at the open window, trying to fancy the air was fresher there. The trees and shrubs of the garden stood stiff and dark; beyond in the roadway a gas-lamp burnt, bright orange against the hazy blue of the evening. Farther were the three lights of the railway signal against the lowering sky. The man and woman spoke to one another in low tones.
>
> "He does not suspect?" said the man, a little nervously.
>
> "Not he," she said peevishly, as though that too irritated her. "He thinks of nothing but the works and the prices of fuel. He has no imagination, no poetry."
>
> "None of these men of iron have," he said sententiously. "They have no hearts."

Immediately, we're in the story. There's a little bit of setup in the brief description of the night, but we're not really sure where we are, what's going on, or who the two people are who begin to speak. We don't know their names or the exact nature of their relationship, but we get the sense that they're having an affair. There's another man involved, probably the man getting cheated on. And we get the sense that the man speaking here is a little full of himself, which is something he might have to pay for later on down the road.

This opening gets our interest precisely because we don't yet know all the details. By infusing the story with an air of mystery, Wells entices us to read on.

Flash Forward   Sometimes in order to really establish what's at stake, you have to start with the finish. Some writers jump to the climax or the conclusion of the story and then work their way backward. The bulk of the tale becomes a "flashback." The advantage of this technique is that you can choose the most dramatic moment of the entire short story and serve it up front and center. The disadvantage is that you've started fooling around with normal chronology, which makes the story less smooth and, at times, less believable.

Flash Forward Beginning in Action   Edgar Allan Poe could do creepy like no one else. Check out the beginning of "The Tell-Tale Heart," an example of the flash forward technique:

> TRUE!—nervous—very, very dreadfully nervous I had been and am; but why will you say that I am mad? The disease had sharpened my senses—not destroyed—not dulled them. Above all was the sense of hearing acute. I heard all things in the heaven and in the earth. I heard many things in hell. How, then, am I mad? Hearken! and observe how healthily—how calmly I can tell you the whole story.
>
> It is impossible to say how first the idea entered my brain; but once conceived, it haunted me day and night. Object there was none. Passion there was none. I loved the old man. He had never wronged me. He had never given me insult. For his gold I had no desire. I think it was his eye! yes, it was this! He had the eye of a vulture—a pale blue eye, with a film over it. Whenever it fell upon me, my blood ran cold; and so by degrees—very gradually—I made up my mind to take the life of the old man, and thus rid myself of the eye forever.

The jittery narrator spills the beans right at the start. We know the old man has been murdered, and we know the narrator did it. When the story continues, we'll flash back to the deed itself. Poe doesn't spoil his climax (the murderer cracks under self-imposed pressure when the cops show up), but he does pick some of his most dramatic material to use for his beginning.

With a hook like this, how can we resist not turning the page? A man has been driven to murder by a motive no greater than an acquaintance's bad eye. This same man claims to hear everything, including broadcasts from hell. By starting us off with a flash forward to murder, Poe repulses us and intrigues us at the same time, and we're compelled to read more.

Try Different Angles

Finding the best entrance to a story is a tricky thing. Think of a lovely courtyard with a big wall around it. The natural entry point is probably the main gate. But it might be more interesting to sledgehammer through the back wall, or tunnel under the side, or be lifted in by a crane. People may appreciate the beauty of the courtyard more if they have to do a little work to get inside. Your short story may operate in a similar way. If readers have to do a little work, they may be more engaged than they would be if you immediately laid out everything they need to know. So try beginning your story one way, then try it from another angle. Soon you'll have a good idea of the best, most compelling way to start.

Find the True Beginning

To find the true beginning of their story, many writers consistently cut off the first 20 percent of their work. The 20 percent is an estimate, not an exact formula; the point is that by removing the throat-clearing at the beginning of your story, you may find that the *real* beginning is a little way into your tale. "Throat-clearing" might include dull, irrelevant background information; unnecessary details about the setting or the scene; or a few broad, sweeping opening lines that call attention to your prowess as a writer rather than to the story itself. Removing the throat-clearing allows the story to start off *firmly*, capturing your readers' attention without hesitation or timidity.

You can inject a lot more mystery and intrigue to a story if you start at an unexpected place. If you're having trouble getting an opening you like, keep clipping off the top of your story. Sometimes the most radical cut is the one that leads to a story's best opening place. For example, look at this potential opening of a short story:

> All my life I'd wanted to be an attorney. I can remember as a kid watching legal dramas on TV and thinking how exciting it would be to stand upon the stage of a courtroom and advocate for justice. The cops, the judges, the jury, the witnesses—all interesting enough in their own way, but none of them captivated me the way the lawyers did. The lawyers were the key actors. They were the ones who really shaped fates.
>
> My first job out of law school was at a mid-sized firm. I worked in the corporate securities department, writing briefs, negotiating,

filing the odd breach of contract suit. Not exactly the stuff of captivating cocktail chatter. It was only when an opening came up in the criminal division that the passion I'd once felt for the law began to reignite within me. I found myself assigned to the division that worked on defenses. The firm handled a lot of *pro bono* cases, work we did for free in order to give a little back to the community. The very first case I tried provided me the fascination with the law I'd long been yearning for.

I could tell he was guilty. It wasn't any great leap of intuition on my part. I could just see it in his hands, the way they fidgeted in his lap when I went over the charges, and then leapt up to his lips when he responded. It was as if he was embarrassed in his physical body and he was trying to make of his hands a filter, narrowing the opening by which the false alibis escaped.

His posture told the story, too. When he described his interactions with the murder victim he leaned way back in the chair, like a cornered animal. He said that the victim had once disrespected him, publicly. I knew what that meant to a kid from the projects. After all, I'd once been such a kid myself. In the projects your reputation was your only source of security. If it was known you could be stepped on, you would be.

In my office, however, the kid seemed small, nervous, and vulnerable. It was an effort to keep reminding myself he was a murderer. Could I be personally responsible for a murderer escaping justice? Walking free out of the courtroom, perhaps to kill again? In all the excitement of my new position, my new life, it appeared suddenly as the most fundamental question. And it was one I'd neglected to ask.

The author chose to start at the start, going all the way back to the narrator's childhood and his early dream of being a lawyer. From there we get some dull material about his first job. Sure, it helps fill in the character, but it's something less than *grabbing*. If we lost those first two paragraphs, would we really be losing all that much? If that back story proves to be essential to this tale, there will be ample opportunities to bring it up later. As the story stands now, the one unique biographical tidbit—the fact that the narrating attorney grew up in the projects—doesn't even come out during the throat-clearing of the first two paragraphs.

As you look at the excerpt, think about the other options for beginning. What if the first two paragraphs were chopped off and the story began at paragraph three? Then the beginning would be, "I could tell he was guilty." That's a lot more intriguing for an opening line. And in losing those first two paragraphs, we get all the more quickly to the dilemma that's going to drive this story—how the narrator is going to be able to justify to himself helping a murderer get off scot-free. In writing your own story, take a hard look at your opening pages. The best spot to start may be hidden well below your first line.

True Beginning in Action Take a look at how Ambrose Bierce begins "An Occurrence at Owl Creek Bridge":

> A man stood upon a railroad bridge in northern Alabama, looking down into the swift water twenty feet below. The man's hands were behind his back, the wrists bound with a cord. A rope closely encircled his neck. It was attached to a stout cross-timber

above his head and the slack fell to the level of his knees. Some loose boards laid upon the sleepers supporting the metals of the railway supplied a footing for him and his executioners—two private soldiers of the Federal army, directed by a sergeant who in civil life may have been a deputy sheriff. At a short remove upon the same temporary platform was an officer in the uniform of his rank, armed. He was a captain. A sentinel at each end of the bridge stood with his rifle in the position known as "support," that is to say, vertical in front of the left shoulder, the hammer resting on the forearm thrown straight across the chest—a formal and unnatural position, enforcing an erect carriage of the body. It did not appear to be the duty of these two men to know what was occurring at the center of the bridge; they merely blockaded the two ends of the foot planking that traversed it.

Bierce chooses to begin this story by focusing on setting. And what a dramatic setting it is: a man standing over a river with a hangman's noose around his neck. In just one paragraph, we get the whole scene. Bierce also uses his opening to establish his authority as a writer. With his careful description of the sentinels' posture, he establishes himself as someone who knows what he's talking about.

Bierce includes other elements of his story in his beginning as well. We get a sense of the straightforward tone of the story to come. We learn the status of the main character, a man about to be hung. At the same time, Bierce clearly conveys what's at stake for this character: unless something turns up quickly, he's going to die. The hanging functions as the inciting incident; it's the reason why the story is being written and the trigger for the action to come. Finally, Bierce has made an effort to hook us in. Why is this man being hung? How will he carry himself in his final minutes? What's going to happen? To answer these questions, we have to read on.

If the author had begun the story with some throat-clearing exposition, we would lose the dramatic impact of this opening. Details such as the condemned man's college, favorite sibling, or political orientation, while relevant to the character, fall outside the narrative constraints of this tale. Another less-true beginning would have been with the main character dead of hanging. It would be a dramatic place to start, yes, but it would undermine the suspense of the potential escape from the gallows. This story at its root is about a man making a mistake and paying for it with his life. The instant before the consequences of his action go into effect is a natural spot to begin. We have a hook, we have stakes, and we have plenty of potential for action. Those are three good signs that the author has found his true beginning.

Find the Ending Place

Deciding how to end your story means much more than figuring out a killer last line. There are two possible places to end your story:

1. Climax
2. Dénouement

You need to think carefully about *where* your story should end before you can figure out the *kind* of ending your story should have.

The main difference between ending with climax or with the dénouement is the extent of the information you provide. In a climax ending, readers must use their imaginations to determine what's to follow. In a dénouement ending, readers get to see firsthand what comes next. Neither mode is better than the other. Ask yourself whether your climactic event provides enough information for you to call it a day. If it does, it may provide your story with an appealingly sudden, or even abrupt, finale. If there's something more you want to indicate, however, you may prefer to complete the untying of the plot with a dénouement.

Climax   Your story has been ticking upward for a while, building to the moment when your problem or conflict gets resolved. That moment is the climax: the turning point in your narrative. Once the upward climb of your story hits the climax, that climb turns into a downward slope that runs down to the ending. Short stories are so concise that many don't even have space for that downward slope. In those cases, the climax, or turning point, also functions as the ending point.

For example, imagine a story about two castaways on a desert island. Their goal is to find a way to get back home to their families. The castaways are from rival countries and speak different languages, but they finally manage to figure out how to cooperate with each other. When the signal fire they've painstakingly built out of coconut shells flares into life, drawing the attention of the passing freighter, we've reached the *climax*. Once that fire's been lit (symbolizing the rivals' ability to work together) and we know everything is going to be okay, the story's over.

Dénouement   The word *dénouement* comes from the Old French for "untying." In writing your story, you've tied a knot for your characters. The dénouement is the place to untangle things. It is the period after the climax that serves as the story's final resolution. It can provide extra information or function as a gentle landing after a bumpy flight. A dénouement is optional: sometimes you won't want anything to detract from the raw power of your climax.

For an example of a dénouement, let's look at our castaways again. Maybe the author was trying to say something about the way enemies can become friends, but only under adverse circumstances. So she might have a little something to add after the climax of the signal fire. The dénouement of the story could show how the two castaways return to being enemies once they reach the safety of the freighter. Or maybe the author has a rosier view of human nature. She could make the freighter crewed by allies of one castaway (and hence enemies of the other). In this version, the dénouement might feature the allied castaway standing up to his countrymen in order to remain loyal to his new friend, the enemy castaway.

Find the True Ending

The type of ending you choose for your story will depend, in part, on *where* you choose to end your story. Ask yourself the following question: *Where in my story* do I want to stop? You may decide to stop at the climax, leaving readers hanging in suspense. Or, you may choose to end after the climax, when things are winding down. Some stories have tidy conclusions that leave no question unanswered; others leave readers with more questions than they had at the start. Deciding how to end your story is often intuitive—an ending just feels right. Sometimes, you may have to try several different types of ending before you land on the one that ends your story on the right note.

When deciding how to end your story, consider the following types of ending:

- Explicit
- Implicit
- Twist
- Tie-back
- Unresolved
- Dialogue and monologue
- Long view

Each type offers something different to your readers and creates a different kind of resolution (or lack thereof).

Explicit An explicit ending tells readers exactly where things stand. For example, if there was a question as to who sunk the yacht or whether the prince was going to pop the question, by the last page of an explicit ending, readers will know the answer. No questions will remain. For example, in "May Day" by F. Scott Fitzgerald, the story ends when the main character, "leaning across the table that held his drawing materials, fired a cartridge into his head just behind the temple." There's no room for confusion in an ending like that.

Explicit Ending in Action Take a look at how the writer Willa Cather handles an explicit ending in her story "Paul's Case":

> The sound of an approaching train woke him, and he started to his feet, remembering only his resolution, and afraid lest he should be too late. He stood watching the approaching locomotive, his teeth chattering, his lips drawn away from them in a frightened smile; once or twice he glanced nervously sidewise, as though he were being watched. When the right moment came, he jumped. As he fell, the folly of his haste occurred to him with merciless clearness, the vastness of what he had left undone. There flashed through his brain, clearer than ever before, the blue of Adriatic water, the yellow of Algerian sands.
>
> He felt something strike his chest,–his body was being thrown swiftly through the air, on and on, immeasurably far and fast, while his limbs gently relaxed. Then, because the picture making mechanism was crushed, the disturbing visions flashed into black, and Paul dropped back into the immense design of things.

Endings don't come much more explicit than this. The main character, Paul, has already been tempted to use a revolver to kill himself. He's put this notion aside, however, and seems to be reconciled to taking the train back to Pittsburgh to face the music. Then suddenly—before we have a chance to brace ourselves—Paul is jumping in front of the train.

From a plot standpoint, there's nothing left to speculate about. From a character standpoint, if there were any lingering ambiguity about Paul or the depth of his resolve, we know now exactly how far he was willing to go. The ending seems believable for the type of person Paul is, and it fits the way he's been behaving. His suicide, however tragic, seems logical. It's almost inevitable.

The suicide is the climax of the story. Since it wraps up all the loose ends, there's no need to drag out the text. A dénouement of the cops coming to investigate, or Paul's father identifying the body, isn't going to tell us anything we don't already know. The author is telling a generally clear-cut story and the clear-cut finish of it has the natural feel of a true ending.

Implicit   When a story has an implicit ending, readers have to do a little work. The answers to the questions in the story are implied, but there may be a lot of room for interpretation. For example, if the main character was trying to work up the nerve to confront a bully, in an implicit ending he may spend the last paragraph forcefully tying his sneakers. Although we're pretty sure he's found the courage he needed, the writer doesn't come right out and tell us. Check out Hemingway's "In Another Country" for an example of an implicit ending. The story ends with a supporting character looking out the window of a rehabilitation center. We have an idea of this character's arc—his wife has just died and he's clearly grieving—but we're left to our own guesswork as far as the narrator is concerned.

Implicit Ending in Action   James Joyce, perhaps one of the greatest writers of the twentieth century, uses an implicit ending in his short story "Araby":

> I lingered before her stall, though I knew my stay was useless, to make my interest in her wares seem the more real. Then I turned away slowly and walked down the middle of the bazaar. I allowed the two pennies to fall against the sixpence in my pocket. I heard a voice call from one end of the gallery that the light was out. The upper part of the hall was now completely dark.
>
> Gazing up into the darkness I saw myself as a creature driven and derided by vanity; and my eyes burned with anguish and anger.

"Araby" begins as a story about a young man with a crush on a girl. His first real contact with her comes when she expresses regret about not being able to attend a bazaar, and he tells her he's going and will bring her something. The story sets us up to expect the resolution of two threads. First, we wonder what the narrator will find for the girl at the fair. Second, we wonder how their relationship will turn out, whether there will indeed be romance. In the end, however, the author resolves neither of these questions.

Even though the bazaar is shutting down at the story's end, we can imagine that the narrator might have every opportunity to speak with the girl the next day, to joke about how he almost bought her a vase. But somehow we know that's now beside the point. The narrator has seen himself as he really is, with all his vanities and illusions exposed. Though Joyce doesn't explicitly resolve the threads of his story, we don't feel like a page is missing when we finish. This is because the story has never really been about its plot points. The arc here isn't a traditional boy-meets-girl. The heart of "Araby" is the narrator's self-discovery. When he recognizes himself as he really is at the end, Joyce rounds off the sense of longing that the story began with. This rounding off of the major subtheme makes the story feel complete, even if the boy's future prospects with the girl remain untold.

The change of focus—from the progress of the narrator's crush on the girl to his recognition of his own failings—comes as a surprise to the reader. This increases the impact of the story. As readers, we didn't see this realization coming, so it delivers a shock just as the narrator has received a shock. Joyce doesn't answer all the plot questions he poses. But in choosing to make his ending implicit, we have a better sense of the "anguish and anger" that surprise his narrator.

Twist A twist ending is a variation of the explicit ending. With a twist, everything you've set up to make readers believe in one view of the world gets turned on its head. The writer O. Henry always liked to end with a surprise, such as in "The Gift of the Magi." In the story, a young wife has cut off her hair to raise money to buy her husband a chain for his watch.

At the end of the story, we learn that the husband has sold his watch to buy combs for his wife's hair. A twist like that can make for a satisfying end to your story. Readers like to feel there's a reason they're investing time in reading. Providing them with a strong impression of irony, as O. Henry does, will help them feel they got something out of the experience of reading. A twist ending also helps provide *closure*. A story like O. Henry's feels completely contained, its ending conclusive. Explicit endings help give a reader a sense of organization, as if swirling scraps of random paper had been put in their proper order and neatly sealed up in a box.

Tie-Back   A tie-back ending connects in some way to the beginning of a story, providing a kicker of sorts. A successful tie-back rounds off the story and provides continuity. For example, a story that begins with a little girl watching volcanic ash destroy a bed of flowers could end weeks later with the girl watching as a new flower breaks through the soot and into the sun. For an excellent tie-back ending, see Kate Chopin's "The Story of an Hour." The lead sentence describes the main character's heart trouble, and in the last sentence it's reported that she's "died of heart disease."

Unresolved   Some stories finish with central conflicts unresolved and questions still unanswered. For example, you might have two horsemen bringing a package to the king across thousands of miles of prairie. Along the way the horsemen may bicker, feud, and ultimately reconcile. At the story's end, we may not see the meeting with the king or even find out what was in the package. It may not matter, however.

The root of a story like this really lies with the characters and their relationship, making the more obvious plot points peripheral. Raymond Carver leaves us with an unresolved ending in his story "The Bath." At the end of the story, the parents don't know who's making the harassing phone calls, nor do they know the medical status of their son, who may or may not be in a coma.

Dialogue and Monologue   You may decide to end your story with characters speaking to each other. Through dialogue, you can sneak in hints of state of mind and emotion that don't come across as clearly in summary. If you don't want an exchange between characters, you may find a single uttered sentence is the best way to cap things off. "A Good Man is Hard to Find" by Flannery O'Connor employs a dialogue ending. The final five lines of the story are an exchange between two supporting characters.

Long View   Some short stories pan way back at the end to provide maximum information. There's no reason you can't jump ahead ten or twenty years for your conclusion, although this device may be better suited to a novel—short stories rarely have the bandwidth to accommodate that much chronological leaping. "Mr. Higginbotham's Catastrophe" by Nathanial Hawthorne has a long-view ending. In the final paragraph, we're shown the main character's favorable marriage and establishment of a manufacturing concern many years later.

Try Different Endings

A good ending should be almost predictable and yet completely unexpected at the same time. In other words, it should make sense within the world of your story, and it shouldn't be dull. What you've set up in the beginning should pay off in the ending, though it's always nice to do so in a way that will surprise your readers—or at least make an impact. By disguising your intentions early on, you may be able to hit readers with something they weren't expecting.

Just as it's helpful to try different angles for beginning a story, experimenting with endings can be valuable. Try it explicit; try it implicit. Try it a week after the climax, or a month, or ten years. The important thing is that you leave your readers with a sense of dramatic satisfaction.

Dramatic Satisfaction Dramatic satisfaction is the state where enough loose ends have been tied up for there to be closure and for readers not to feel shortchanged. If readers are worried that they haven't been given the final page or pages of a story, they're not going to be satisfied. If they feel like things fit together and that the dramatic elements of the piece have been resolved, however, they'll put your story down feeling that their time was well spent.

To be dramatically satisfying, a piece doesn't neces- sarily have to wrap itself up neatly in a bow. Sometimes the best endings are the ones where the heroes don't clearly overcome the villains and ride off into the sunset. In a story with just such an implicit ending, character often drives the action. The character's changes may provide more of the sense of dramatic satisfaction than the resolution of the major plot points.

True Ending in Action Take a look at how Ambrose Bierce ends "An Occurrence at Owl Creek Bridge":

> Doubtless, despite his suffering, he had fallen asleep while walking, for now he sees another scene—perhaps he has merely recovered from a delirium. He stands at the gate of his own home. All is as he left it, and all bright and beautiful in the morning sunshine. He must have traveled the entire night. As he pushes open the gate and passes up the wide white walk, he sees a flutter of female garments; his wife, looking fresh and cool and sweet, steps down from the veranda to meet him. At the bottom of the steps she stands waiting, with a smile of ineffable joy, an attitude of matchless grace and dignity. Ah, how beautiful she is! He springs forward with extended arms. As he is about to clasp her he feels a stunning blow upon the back of the neck; a blinding white light blazes all about him with a sound like the shock of a cannon—then all is darkness and silence!
>
> Peyton Farquhar was dead; his body, with a broken neck, swung gently from side to side beneath the timbers of the Owl Creek bridge.

With this ending, there's nothing more to be said, nothing left to resolve. The main character introduced on the railroad bridge with a noose around his neck has hanged to death. The climax and the true ending are one and the same here. A dénouement would only have lessened the impact. We don't need to read about the coffin, or the dead man's family's grief, or the next phase in the war. Short stories are self-contained units, and this story is limited to one man's hanging. As soon as this is resolved, the story needs to end.

"An Occurrence at Owl Creek Bridge" features a great example of a twist ending. For the bulk of the story, we've followed along with Farquhar's narrow evasion of a certain death. Then, at the threshold of the longed-for reunion, Bierce gives us a nasty shock: the escape was a dream. The pressure on Farquhar's neck, the sensation of spinning, his swollen tongue—which initially seemed to be part of the experience of the getaway—are revealed as the impressions of a man being hung. The story of a miracle has become the story of a routine execution.

Exercises

- Take a look at a short story you've written. If you don't yet have one, write one! Try cutting off the first sentence, then the first two sentences, until you've cut off around 20 percent of your story. How does your beginning look now? Have you found the true beginning? Try starting your story here, further in, rather than where you originally planned to start.

- Consider the ending of a story you've written. If you don't yet have one, write one. Try to identify the type—explicit, implicit, twist, etc. Now rewrite the ending so that you use a different type. Then rewrite it again, using another type. What is your true ending?

- Briefly sketch out the beginning of a short story. Then try to start the same story from the ending point of the sketch.

Effective Description

Thorough description is one of your most useful tools as a writer. Description allows you to apply color, texture, and dimension to your story, particularly to scene and setting. Have you ever heard the expression "set the scene"? Setting the scene means you present a situation vividly and fully so that your readers feel like they're part of it. How skillfully you render your descriptions will often determine how well readers imagine your story. But what constitutes *effective* description? How much is *too* much? Knowing some techniques for creating lively descriptions will help make your story come alive.

A laundry list of details may paint an accurate picture, but that picture is useless if it puts your readers to sleep. Effective description hones in on *specific, relevant* details that really illuminate the story. Those details can be few or many. Ernest Hemingway was brilliant at writing spare but stunning descriptions. The French writer Marcel Proust, on the other hand, could spend pages describing the stalk of a flower until it took on hallucinatory proportions. The level of detail you provide will depend on your voice and how relevant the details are to your story.

6

Be Hi-Def

A great short story presents a unique situation and memorable characters—but the fact is that after thousands of years of writing and countless stories, every story has probably been told already. The only path to fresh material is in the *details*. Strong description allows *readers* to see and experience a story as if they were witnessing it themselves—and as though this were the first time this story has ever been told.

The key to vivid description is *hi-def details*. Honing in on the specifics of a character, scene, or setting will make it more lucid. Unspecific description, on the other hand, is often vague and forgettable. Take *a look* at these two examples, in which we try to describe a city:

> The city was almost empty at that time of year.

> In January, Reykjavik's café windows gaped like a skeleton's eye sockets, and the streets themselves seemed to shiver as the wind sped over the unscarred snow.

The second example is more engaging because it *shows* clear, specific details about the city that gives us a sense of how empty it is, rather than simply *telling* us that it's empty. It's almost always better to show rather than tell. Skillful description employs details that speak volumes about the person, place, thing, or time that is being described.

Avoid Dead Language

Writing compelling description is like pruning a tree. To keep it healthy, you have to get rid of the dead foliage. Similarly, to keep your writing lively, you must get rid of the dead language. It's your job as a writer to cast a fresh eye on even common place objects and situations. To do that, you must avoid overused or clichéd language. Consider these two examples:

> Jeannie was as pretty as a princess.

> Jeannie carried herself as if she had a textbook balanced on her head. Her piercing green eyes seemed to take in every person in the room at the same time. She was ninth grade's answer to royalty.

The first example relies on a common cliché—*pretty as a princess*—to suggest that this character is attractive. Because it's a cliché, it's forgettable—and it doesn't help us *see* the character. All it tells us is that the author wants us to think that Jeannie is attractive. The second example is more vivid and engaging because it describes the *qualities* that make Jeannie attractive without resorting to predictable or overused language. More important, we not only learn that Jeanie is attractive but that she possesses characteristics that make her princesslike. It's a much richer description.

Use Action Verbs

Many young writers assume that effective description involves endless strings of adjectives. Actually, the opposite is true. Too many adjectives can dilute your descriptions, making them cluttered and clumsy. Well-chosen action verbs, on the other hand, are vital to effective description. As the name suggests, action verbs demonstrate *action*, so they are particularly useful when you need to describe something that is happening in a scene. Let's look at a few examples:

WEAK: Tina's laugh was loud, cackling, and cacophonous.
STRONG: Tina *brayed* like a donkey.

WEAK: The buzz of the alarm clock was loud, fuzzy, and shrill.
STRONG: The alarm clock *buzzed* like a bumblebee on steroids.

WEAK: Pedro looked irritated, exasperated, and annoyed.
STRONG: Pedro *bristled* like a mad cat.

Notice that in the first two weak examples, a "verb of being" was used: *was*. Verbs of being (also called "to be" verbs) aren't useful for description because they indicate a state of being, not an action. The weak examples are also redundant: the strings of adjectives describe similar qualities. The adjectives are *synonyms*. As a result, each successive adjective has less impact.

The improved, strong sentences include action verbs. Each verb paints a clear, arresting picture of the action and leaves us with a striking impression of the character or object that is being described.

Avoid Fake and Fancy

One very common misconception about description is that it's supposed to be fancy, full of long sentences stuffed with SAT words. Nothing could be further from the truth. The best writing is *clear* writing, writing that gives readers a clear mental image of what's going on in the story. Compare these two descriptions:

> As Rodger disembarked the contraption, I formulated a question in my mind to ascertain his current condition. On his approach, I inquired about the ride.
>
> "Rodger," I asked. "Did you enjoy your ride on the roller coaster?"
>
> Rodger looked bilious, queasy, and pallid. He walked without haste to the rickety oak bench that sat ten feet from the roller coaster exit. He sat down gradually and languidly. I noticed that he seemed unhealthy and indisposed, his skin a faint emerald color, like spinach, but not as dark.

> "How was the rollercoaster?" I asked.
>
> Rodger sat down slowly on the bench near the exit. I noticed he had turned a faint shade of asparagus green and seemed to have lost some of his interest in life.

The first description has lots of big words and SAT-worthy adjectives, but something isn't quite right. First, no one actually talks this way. Since this isn't a nineteenth-century Victorian novel, the language seems pretentious and clunky. The writer seems to be more interested in impressing us with his vocabulary than with rendering a clear, compelling scene. The second example flows naturally, with straightforward language that doesn't get in the way of the scene. As a result, it is not only clearer, it's shorter—and funnier. And the reader gets it right away.

Visualize Your Location

Once you know what happens in your story and whom it happens to, you have to think about exactly where and when it happens. A well-imagined setting provides the background in front of which your story unfolds.

Imagine you're planning a trip, and you're trying to decide where to go. Maybe you want to go somewhere warm. That's a good start—but many places are warm. But you want to surf on your trip, which makes it a little clearer. You need somewhere near water, and you need somewhere conducive to surfing—such as Hawaii or California. You consider your options and narrow them down until you decide exactly what location will meet your needs, wants, and budget. When you select a location for your story, you'll use the same sort of thought process. Your setting can't be just anywhere in general. It must be a *specific place* at a *specific time*. Visualizing it clearly is a vital step to creating a realistic, detailed setting.

Enrich Your Setting

Location is only one element of setting. When you develop your setting more fully, there are a lot of things you need to keep in mind: where the location is exactly, what it looks like, how it smells, how it sounds, who inhabits it, and how it feels to be there. These are all *elements* of the setting, which include:

- **Time period (past, present, future):** Mississippi in the 1800s; Rochester, New York, during the Great Depression; New York City in 2020
- **Time of day:** just before the sun rises; in twilight; at high noon
- **Weather:** the worst blizzard of the winter; a perfect spring day
- **Social atmosphere:** wartime; the days leading up to a presidential election
- **Economic conditions:** the Great Depression; a boom economy; post-internet-bust recession

When you pay close attention to the specific setting in which your characters are living, you'll be able to create a more realistic, vivid, energetic story. Your characters will be more believable if the world they live in is specifically drawn.

You should have all the details of your setting in your mind before you start to write. You'll probably come up with these details when you plan out your story in your writing journal—this is your place to brainstorm, free write, and really think about your setting. Not every detail will make it into your story, but each will *inform* your story and make you seem authoritative as a writer.

Select Useful Details

The trick to establishing your setting is figuring out which details best serve your story. You don't need to describe *everything*. That would get dull. It's better if you focus on the parts that are necessary or *relevant*. For example, if you're writing a story about racial conditions in the South in the 1950s, you'd probably focus your description on the time period, the social atmosphere, and economic conditions. Those details would help illuminate the codes of behavior that your story is exploring. However, if you're writing a story that takes place on a deserted island and we need to know only that the island is deserted and remote, you might not have to give a lot of detail about where the island is exactly. You could concentrate on describing the island itself and why it is dangerous or beautiful.

Keep in mind that story settings are not always unique. In fact, some settings are deliberately generic. Let's say, for example, that you are writing a story about life in an average American small town. You'd probably choose to focus on details that make the town appear to be just like any other small town (the main street, the town square, and the local barber shop, for example). Simultaneously, you would probably *avoid* details that give the town too much individuality. Even the name might be generic, such as Springfield. By focusing on your setting's purpose, you'll develop a better sense for which elements and details should and shouldn't be included in your descriptions.

Selecting Details in Action   James Joyce, one of the greatest writers of the twentieth century, ends his short story "The Dead" with an evocative description:

> A few light taps upon the pane made him turn to the window. It had begun to snow again. He watched sleepily the flakes, silver and dark, falling obliquely against the lamplight. The time had come for him to set out on his journey westward. Yes, the newspapers were right: snow was general all over Ireland. It was falling on every part of the dark central plain, on the treeless hills, falling softly upon the Bog of Allen and, farther westward, softly falling into the dark mutinous Shannon waves. It was falling, too, upon every part of the lonely churchyard on the hill where Michael Furey lay buried. It lay thickly drifted on the crooked crosses and headstones, on the spears of the little gate, on the barren thorns. His soul swooned slowly as he heard the snow falling faintly through the universe and faintly falling, like the descent of their last end, upon all the living and the dead.

The writing in this final paragraph is beautiful, and it creates a melancholy atmosphere. The element Joyce renders so poetically—the snow falling—has a powerful effect on the story's protagonist, Gabriel. Snow is falling all over Ireland. It will fall on Gabriel as he travels, just it is falling on the grave of his wife's former lover. Joyce's description suggests that the snow, not unlike death, touches everything and everyone, from the "dark central plain" to the "lonely churchyard." In the shadowy lamplight, the snow becomes much more than just an element of the weather. Gabriel's "soul [swoons] slowly" as he hears the snow "falling faintly through the universe." Joyce has not only rendered a beautiful description of snow falling, but he also has turned an element of the weather into an agent for a new awareness, connecting Gabriel to his wife's past, and "all the living and the dead." He has made his description of the setting useful to the story.

Set the Mood

Detailed elements of setting create a believable world for your story, but they also do something else: they establish the *atmosphere* for your story. Atmosphere is just as important as the setting itself because it dictates the *mood* of the setting and the story. Setting and atmosphere go hand in hand; you can't have one without the other. Changing an element of your setting can have a big effect on atmosphere. Consider these two descriptions:

A beach in summer. It's 82 degrees, in the early afternoon. The sun is shining. Waves are crashing on the coast, as people in swimsuits sunbathe on the hot sand. Roller bladers roll along the boardwalk, where local merchants and artisans sell their wares. Hungry beachgoers pack the sidewalk cafes. Not far away, a pier bustles with families who wait in line to play games and ride bumper cars and the Ferris wheel.

> A winter day on the same beach. It's overcast, and the offshore winds make it seem much colder than the 43 degrees outside. With the exception of a few intrepid dog walkers, the beach is empty; it feels almost abandoned. The shops that line the boardwalk are boarded up for the winter, and the pier is closed for the season, creating a kind of amusement park ghost town.

Notice that when we change one element of the setting—in this case, the season—the atmosphere changes drastically. The location is the same, but the mood has taken a 180-degree turn. It's easy to imagine two completely different stories taking place in the same location because certain elements of the setting and the atmosphere have changed so much.

Setting and Atmosphere in Action In the story "At the Bay," Katherine Mansfield establishes the setting and atmosphere from the opening paragraph:

> Very early morning. The sun was not yet risen, and the whole of Crescent Bay was hidden under a white sea-mist. The big bush-covered hills at the back were smothered. You could not see where they ended and the paddocks and bungalows began. The sandy road was gone and the paddocks and bungalows the other side of it; there were no white dunes covered with reddish grass beyond them; there was nothing to mark which was beach and where was the sea. A heavy dew had fallen. The grass was blue. Big drops hung on the bushes and just did not fall; the silvery, fluffy toi-toi was limp on its long stalks, and all the marigolds and the pinks in the bungalow gardens were bowed to the earth with wetness.

Drenched were the cold fuchsias, round pearls of dew lay on the flat nasturtium leaves. It looked as though the sea had beaten up softly in the darkness, as though one immense wave had come rippling, rippling—how far? Perhaps if you had waked up in the middle of the night you might have seen a big fish flicking in at the window and gone again . . .

Three important elements of setting come into play right away: location, time, and weather. We know it's early morning, at a bay, which is covered in mist. Mansfield makes clear which of these features is most important by cleverly describing the bay in terms of the thick mist and moisture that blanket it. We learn that the mist has "smothered" the hills and covered the "whole of Crescent Bay." It's as if the sandy road is "gone" and there are no "white dunes covered with reddish grass beyond them." The mist is matched by a "heavy dew" with "big drops" that drench the vegetation. Mansfield's description suggests that this is no ordinary morning mist. It's as if the sea had "beaten up" into an "immense wave" that rippled over the bay the night before. We can almost hear the silence of the scene; we half-expect something magical to rise out of that mist like we imagine would happen in a fairy tale. Mansfield lays an effective groundwork for the story by rendering a bay that seems almost enchanted by the mist that envelops it.

List Fifty Things

To enrich the description of your setting, try an exercise called "Fifty Things I Know." Imagine that you are in the

scene of your story. Make a list of fifty things you see there.
Be extremely detailed. For example, say your scene is in a
diner. Your list might look something like this:

1. Linoleum-topped tables
2. A neon sign outside the window with a broken "D," so
   it's an "iner"
3. A heaping plate with a massive burger on it
4. A broken coffeepot
5. A stack of coffee cups on the counter
6. A half of a chocolate cake under a glass dome
7. Coffee rings on the tables
8. Crumbs under the chairs
9. Cheerios scattered over the table from the family who
   just left
10. Water spots on the windows
11. A few loose coins on the counter
12. A forgotten glove placed in plain view on the counter
13. A water-wrinkled flyer on the front door announcing a
    Little League meeting
14. Chairs with metal legs
15. Large pane windows
16. A short-order cook peeking from the kitchen door
17. A swinging door that separates dining room from kitchen
18. A table of teenage girls drinking Cokes
19. A young man reading a newspaper at the counter
20. A flickering fluorescent light
21. A bell over the front door
22. A red string the bell hangs from
23. Balled-up wrapping paper left underneath a chair

24. Ice melting in a few forgotten glasses

25. Stacked plastic cups

26. Bins of silverware

27. Balled-up napkins on a table

28. A dishpan of dirty plates near the kitchen door

29. Some dollar bills on an empty table

30. Rectangular napkin dispensers

31. A shelf of wooden crafts for sale near the cash register

32. A jar for coins, with a sign that says "Help Billy"

33. A lost-cat flyer posted on the cash register

34. A BLT waiting to be carried to a table

35. An order of French fries next to the BLT

36. Bottles of ketchup waiting on a tray to be refilled

37. A spare order pad tucked under the cash register

38. A sign in the window that says "OPEN"

39. A black bag-lined trash can behind the counter

40. A dirty welcome mat by the front door

41. A bottle of cleaning fluid on a shelf by the kitchen door

42. A high chair in the corner

43. Several booster seats stacked up in the back

44. A coatrack with some metal hangers hanging on it

45. A stack of free local newspapers on the windowsill

46. Duct tape over a crack in the glass in the front door

47. A refrigerator holding cans of soda and bottled water

48. A few ashtrays along the counter

49. A mop and bucket behind the counter

50. A picture of the owner's daughter taped to the cash register

Do whatever you have to do to get to fifty things. It will seem like a lot, but this exercise will force you to truly see the world of your story.

Once you've done this, strip the list down to the ten or twenty things that really stand out. For example, in the above list, you could probably eliminate things like the tables, the chairs, and the stacks of coffee cups. They don't tell you anything new, and they're nothing you wouldn't expect in a diner. But there are some interesting, unique details there as well. We'd keep the following things:

1. The broken sign
2. The broken coffeepot
3. A heaping plate with a massive burger on it
4. The forgotten glove
5. A shelf of wooden crafts for sale near the cash register
6. A jar for coins, with a sign that says "Help Billy"
7. A stack of free local newspapers on the windowsill
8. Duct tape over a crack in the glass in the front door
9. The picture of the owner's daughter
10. Balled-up wrapping paper left underneath a chair

These details show us things about the diner. For example, the broken sign and the broken coffeepot suggest that this is not a fancy, upscale place. The picture and the forgotten glove show that this is a friendly, local place where people care about one another. The wrapping paper under the chair suggests that a celebration of some kind has just taken place—there might be a story there. Also think about keeping details that are slightly contradictory. In the above list, there's a heaping plate of food. Perhaps the diner is poor, but the portions (and therefore the owners) are generous. Well-chosen details can make your setting rich and complex.

Description in Action   Ambrose Bierce makes clever use of description to hint at his main character's circumstances in "An Occurrence at Owl Creek Bridge." Check out the following passage:

> At last he found a road which led him in what he knew to be the right direction. It was as wide and straight as a city street, yet it seemed untraveled. No fields bordered it, no dwelling anywhere. Not so much as the barking of a dog suggested human habitation. The black bodies of the trees formed a straight wall on both sides, terminating on the horizon in a point, like a diagram in a lesson in perspective. Overhead, as he looked up through this rift in the wood, shone great garden stars looking unfamiliar and grouped in strange constellations. He was sure they were arranged in some order which had a secret and malign significance. The wood on either side was full of singular noises, among which—once, twice, and again—he distinctly heard whispers in an unknown tongue.
>
> His neck was in pain and lifting his hand to it found it horribly swollen. He knew that it had a circle of black where the rope had bruised it. His eyes felt congested; he could no longer close them. His tongue was swollen with thirst; he relieved its fever by thrusting it forward from between his teeth into the cold air. How softly the turf had carpeted the untraveled avenue—he could no longer feel the roadway beneath his feet!

Bierce is describing a man's flight from his own hanging. Or is he? A close reading of the details suggests that Bierce is up to something else. The character begins by walking down a road that is "untraveled" and without "human habitation"—a sort of ghost road. The trees form "black bodies." He sees stars that group into "strange constellations." Every detail implies a kind of exalted, almost surreal terrain. The description suggests that the character is traveling, but we don't know the terrain. It's as though he's navigating some kind of netherworld.

Bierce's intention becomes more explicit in the second paragraph. At first glance, the details in this passage make perfect sense. His "neck was in pain" and is "horribly swollen"—from being hanged, we assume. That seems logical, but then we learn that the character's eyes are "congested" and that he can't close them. Also, his tongue is swollen, and it's thrust "between his teeth into the cold air." Further, he can no longer feel the ground beneath his feet. Rather than describing a man who has escaped hanging, these characteristics actually describe someone who is *dead*. Without *telling* us that the character is dead, Bierce paints a picture of a dead man having one final daydream. In this way, the passage not only describes the character's situation, it foreshadows the story's surprise ending.

Exercises

• Write a one-paragraph description of your room. Elaborate on details that reflect your personality, and leave out those that do not.

- Write a one-paragraph description of your best friend. Try to include only the details about your friend that reveal his or her specific personality.

- Write a few sentences describing the setting for an ideal vacation place. Remember to include details about the elements of setting, such as time of day, weather, economic conditions, and social atmosphere.

Dialogue

A few lines of conversation, carefully chosen and skillfully placed, can often have more impact than pages of description. While readers may tolerate poorly executed description, they probably will not tolerate fake-sounding dialogue. As with other aspects of a short story such as description, character development, and point of view, writing great dialogue is a skill you can learn. A good ear, keen listening skills, and a sense for the way different people talk will help you to write strong dialogue that fits your story.

Short story dialogue is not simply a transcription of people talking—in fact, it's not much like "real" talking at all. Always remember that a short story is a very small, carefully chosen slice of experience. Stories are not word-for-word records of everything the characters say. Your job is to imagine and record *affecting* and *revealing* conversations between your characters. Each scene of dialogue should move the story forward and help to expose your characters more fully to your reader. In other words, dialogue must serve a distinct purpose, especially in a short story where economy counts.

7

Know the Functions

Dialogue serves multiple functions in a short story. When you begin writing dialogue, think about what you want to accomplish in that scene. Good dialogue serves your story in several different ways:

- **Reveals character and establishes relationships:** Conversations can be a powerful tool for revealing your characters and their relationship dynamics. A short, well-written scene can sometimes convey more than a chapter of description.

- **Provides exposition:** Dialogue can function the same way as expository prose. Instead of the story's narrator explaining a given situation, the character does the explaining. The trick is to write conversations that tell the reader something new.

- **Conveys a sense of place and time:** Similar to exposition, two or more characters establish the time and place of a story through their conversation rather than through expository prose.

- **Establishes and develops conflict:** Maybe no device is as effective for establishing conflict as dialogue. Conflict is the clash or opposition of characters' desires, and dialogue allows characters to verbalize that tension. In extreme cases, a conversation between characters will express conflict directly. In most cases, though, conflict is expressed more indirectly, through subtext.

Drive the Intention

Just as people act with intention, people speak with intention. Whether they are rhapsodizing about pop music to impress a date or just talking to kill an uncomfortable silence, people speak with intent. Just as motivation drives characters' actions, motivation compels them to speak. If you know your characters' motivations, you will not only know

what they want but also you'll have a clearer notion what
they will say to get it. Motivations are not always explicit,
and sometimes dialogue expresses a person's intentions
more indirectly. Either way, something must be driving the
dialogue.

Intention in Action Take a look at the following scene
of dialogue, in which each character has a different intention
for saying what she says:

> "Joan, we need to talk about your grades," said Joan's mother.
>
> "Would you pass the salt?" Joan asked.
>
> "They've been slipping recently."
>
> "This lasagna is delicious."
>
> "Joan, if you don't raise your grades, you'll have to give up softball."
>
> "Fine. May I be excused?"

In this short scene, Joan's mother's intentions are clear. She
is concerned about her daughter's grades, and she wants
Joan to improve them. Joan's comments are not quite as
direct, but we can infer a lot about her motivations from
her replies. When Joan's mother addresses the issue of her
grades, Joan asks for the salt. When her mother persists, Joan
tries to change the subject. She doesn't want to talk about
her grades. When her mother gives her an ultimatum, Joan
immediately asks to leave the table. Joan doesn't express
anger or irritation explicitly, but it's clear that she is upset with
her mother's final comment, and she wants to end the conversation. The characters' opposing motivations fuel the scene and
illuminate a conflict between them.

Be Genuine

Dialogue often gives readers a clue to how experienced a writer is. Good dialogue seems to naturally fit characters' personalities and comes across as a genuine conversation. It also has a function and somehow propels the story forward. Amateurish dialogue sounds distinctly unlike the way people actually talk, and it seems pointless or irrelevant to the story. Consider this conversation between two friends:

> "Good morning, Tom, how are you today?"
>
> "I am well, Steve. How are you?"
>
> "I am fine. I trust your dog is well."
>
> "My dog is well, Tom. Thank you for you asking. How is your dog?"

First, people don't really talk like that, much less two friends, so this conversation seems odd and a little creepy. Both characters are painfully polite, and both use almost formal language. Unless your story is set in a highly formal atmosphere, such as a thirteenth-century coronation, two friends probably wouldn't interact this way. As a result, this conversation lacks a sense of authenticity. In order to write dialogue that rings true, you'll need to hone your ear for real conversations. Take a look at how the stilted exchange between Tom and Steve might sound in more genuinely written dialogue:

> "Hey, Tom—what's up?"
>
> "Not much. Haven't seen you in a while."

"How's the dog?"

"Doing great. Learned to catch a Frisbee. How's yours?"

This exchange is probably still too mundane to make it into a story—but at least it sounds more like two people talking normally.

Transcription   In order to write good, natural dialogue, you need to pay attention to the way people actually speak. A well-known and very useful writing exercise is to tape a conversation and then transcribe it—that is, write it out word for word. Don't change anything. Note the pauses, the stammering, the *ums* and the *uhs*. This is hard work, but it's one of the best ways to learn speech patterns and to get a sense of how people actually communicate with one another. You'll probably notice certain verbal tendencies that most people have in common, such as using contractions, slang, tone, and sentence structure. You can draw from such observations when you begin writing dialogue for your story.

Dialogue vs. Real Speech   It's essential to remember that dialogue—even the most authentic dialogue—is *not* real speech. A good writer doesn't just duplicate the way people talk. Think about your transcribed conversation: this is not story material. It's not snappy, intriguing, or even especially interesting. The truth is, a lot of *real* speech is boring. Long pauses, *ums* and *hmms*, repetitions, silly phrases, and clichés are all a part of real speech. Good writers compose dialogue to give the *illusion* of real speech, while avoiding all the less compelling (or downright boring) aspects of actual conversation.

For example, people often repeat themselves. In a short story, you don't have space for needless repetition, so you would only include repetition in dialogue if it served to reveal a relevant aspect of the character or to reinforce the story's established rhythm. Similarly, a character's verbal tic or habit (like saying "um" a lot or adding "you know?" to the end of every sentence) might be genuine, but it can distract from the content of the dialogue. As a writer, you'll need to use your best judgment to balance genuine dialogue with the demands of efficient and effective storytelling.

Create Speech Patterns

Each character in your story has a particular voice. Finding the individual voice for each character will lend your dialogue variety and help make each scene more engaging. That doesn't mean that you should make everyone sound weird or eccentric. Just be aware that all characters don't sound the same. Your characters' speech patterns will vary, and you should aim to draw out and highlight that variety. It will serve as a spice for your dialogue and help lead you to places where two characters might diverge or conflict. There are three aspects of dialogue that you can play with to create variety:

- Diction
- Syntax
- Verbal tics and habits

Diction *Merriam Webster's Collegiate Dictionary* defines *diction* as "choice of words especially with regard to correctness, clearness, or effectiveness." Your diction is your own personal vocabulary. Think of it as a verbal fingerprint. While people might share a similar diction (members of the same family, for example), it usually differs from person to person. That difference can be obvious or very subtle. Diction is affected by upbringing, region, personality, social environment, and peers.

Syntax *Syntax* simply means word order, or the way a person arranges words to form phrases and clauses. Syntax indicates a lot about a character. For example, most native English speakers share a similar syntax. That is, they generally follow the same word order patterns. Native Italian speakers, on the other hand, share a very different syntax; their word order pattern is different. When writing dialogue, considering your character's syntax could help give your dialogue more variety.

Verbal Tics and Habits Idiosyncrasies are what make us individuals. Just as people have idiosyncratic physical habits, such as biting their nails or tapping their feet, they also have personal verbal tics. A tic might be an inflection, a repeated word, or a phrase they like so much they apply it to all kinds of circumstances. We all have verbal habits that we've formed over time; they are extensions of personality.

For example:

- "Yadda yadda yadda"
- "Ya know?"
- "I mean . . ."
- "It's like . . ."
- "Absolutely."

As you write dialogue, think about your characters' personalities and whether or not they have any noticeable verbal tics or habits. Remember that certain verbal habits (a character who interjects "like" into every sentence, for example) can be just as distracting as they are illuminating, so choose wisely, and don't overdo it.

Speech Patterns in Action Let's take a look at how diction, syntax, and verbal tics and habits come into play in two different scenes of dialogue. Take a look at this passage from "The Notorious Jumping Frog of Calaveras County" by Mark Twain:

> The feller took the box again, and took another long, particular look, and give it back to Smiley, and says, very deliberate, "Well, I don't see no p'ints about that frog that's any better'n any other frog."
>
> "Maybe you don't," Smiley says. "Maybe you understand frogs, and maybe you don't understand ëem; maybe you've had experience, and maybe you an't only a amature, as it were. Anyways, I've got *my* opinion, and I'll risk forty dollars that he can outjump any frog in Calaveras county."
>
> And the feller studied a minute, and then says, kinder sad like,

> "Well, I'm only a stranger here, and I an't got no frog; but if I had a
> frog, I'd bet you."

Notice how Twain uses rural diction—"p'nts" and "better'n,"
for example—to lend his characters authenticity. Both men
in the scene have a similar verbal habit of clipping their
words; they say "em" instead of "them," and "a'nt" instead
of "ain't." We get the feeling that these men probably aren't
well educated. And while their syntax is fairly straightforward, Twain makes good use of double negatives to stay true
to his chararcter's speech ("I don't see no p'ints . . ." and "I
an't got no frog . . .").

Now compare the diction in Twain's scene to the proper
English spoken by the characters in Henry James's long story
"Daisy Miller":

> "The young girl is very pretty," said Winterbourne in a moment.
>
> "Of course she's pretty. But she is very common."
>
> "I see what you mean, of course," said Winterbourne after
> another pause.
>
> "She has that charming look that they all have," his aunt
> resumed. "I can't think where they pick it up; and she dresses in
> perfection—no, you don't know how well she dresses. I can't think
> where they get their taste."
>
> "But, my dear aunt, she is not, after all, a Comanche savage."
>
> "She is a young lady," said Mrs. Costello, "who has an intimacy
> with her mamma's courier."

In contrast to Twain's characters, James's characters speak
perfect English. We can infer that they are probably well

educated and part of the upper class. Unlike the verbal tics and habits that mark Twain's dialogue, the speech here is more notable for its propriety. Each character speaks in complete sentences, with a standard syntax. With this kind of dialogue, James depicts a rarefied and snobby world, where breeding and propriety are paramount.

Show, Don't Tell

One function of dialogue is to provide exposition. But it's important not to insult your reader's intelligence by lining your dialogue with obvious explanation. Like good description, good dialogue *shows* instead of *tells*. Consider this example:

> "I think you are annoyed with me," she said.
>
> "Yes, I am annoyed with you," he said.

We know that one character is annoyed with the other—because the writer *tells* us so. But the impact of the exchange is diminished because the scene doesn't *show* that annoyance. We cannot see or feel the character's irritation, so it's less dramatic and less engaging. Now consider this example:

> He jerked his head away as she tried to fix his hair.
>
> "What's wrong?" she asked.
>
> "Nothing!" he said.

Nowhere in this short scene does the character say or even acknowledge that he is annoyed, yet his irritation is obvious from this interaction. Not only that, we can almost feel it. It doesn't need to be said or explained because the scene *shows* it. Beyond that, the scene also encourages us to infer, which helps to actively engage us in the scene. Finally, the scene rings much more true to human interaction. People often don't verbally acknowledge their own feelings and motives in the middle of a conversation. Trying to explain and tell too much will weaken your dialogue.

Create Subtext

Subtext is the unspoken thoughts and motives of your characters—what they really think, believe, and feel. Think of it as the *unspoken* dialogue. In a well-written scene, subtext rarely cracks the surface of the dialogue, except in moments of intense conflict. Rather, it rumbles underneath and causes tremors in the conversation. Take a look at the following scene in a school cafeteria. It shows what two high school students say to each other—and what are really thinking when they say it:

"Hi," she said.
(What she's thinking: *Oh, God, that was way too cheery.*)

"Hey," he said and smiled.
(What he's thinking: *She's talking to me. I hope my breath doesn't stink.*)

"Casserole today?"
(What she's thinking: *He's so cute. I hope my hair looks okay.*)

"Yeah, terrible as always."

(What he's thinking: *Why haven't I noticed her before?*)

"I'm Jordana," she said almost with a cringe.

(What she's thinking: *I hate my stupid name.*)

"Cool hair," he said and smiled.

(What he's thinking: *What an awesome name.*)

This scene, though pretty dull, clearly demonstrates the idea of subtext. As a writer, you should be able to write the spoken dialogue between two characters *as well as* be fully aware of the subtext. Despite the fact that the subtext may only be implied, it will add layers of depth and complexity to your scene. It will also make each of the character's motives clearer as they interact with each other.

Use the "Iceberg" Principle

In his book *Death in the Afternoon*, Ernest Hemingway writes, "If a writer of prose knows enough about what he is writing about he may omit things that he knows and the reader, if the writer is writing truly enough, will have a feeling of those things as strongly as though the writer had stated them. The dignity of movement of an iceberg is due to only one-eighth of it being above water." Hemingway believed that, like an iceberg, 80 percent of a short story is "underwater." That is, most of what really happens in a short story cannot be seen on the page. Rather, it's implied or hinted at by subtext or descriptive details provided by the writer. As a writer, you should be just as familiar with the hidden "80 percent" of unspoken details and dialogue as you are with the language rendered on the page. As you sharpen your skills, the words that are not said in a scene will become just as powerful as those that are.

Use Simple Tags

A *dialogue tag* is the attribution that usually follows a line of dialogue. For example, "he said," "Andrew said," and "said the creepy man" are all dialogue tags. The tag can precede or follow dialogue, and it may not always be necessary if it is clear who is speaking. You should err on the side of simplicity when choosing your dialogue tags. In this case, creative isn't always better. Think of it this way: tags shouldn't upstage your actual dialogue; they should serve only to make the dialogue clearer. The best tags are simple and direct, such as the following:

- Said
- Replied
- Answered

These tags identify the speaker without calling too much attention to themselves, and they express simply what is happening: someone is speaking, replying, or answering. That leaves the reader free to focus on the dialogue itself.

Accuracy When using a dialogue tag, make sure your word choice is accurate. Many writers make the mistake of believing that any action verb can serve as a dialogue tag.

Consider the following example:

"I've been eating eels," she laughed.

This tag is relatively simple, but there's one major problem: *laughing* is not *saying*. Laughing is a different physical act. The word choice is inaccurate. If the writer wants to suggest that the character is laughing at herself or at her own comment, a better option would be to write a separate sentence:

"I've been eating eels." She laughed and shook her head in disbelief.

The writer still makes it clear who's speaking, but we now get an accurate description of what's happening physically.

Adverbs   Adding adverbs to dialogue tags is a common impulse among new writers. In good dialogue, however, these adverbs are often unnecessary or repetitive. Effective dialogue conveys a character's implications and tone *within* the lines themselves. The reader can infer the tone of the characters from the content, context, and punctuation. Consider these examples:

"My pants are on fire!" he said loudly.
"My pants are on fire!" he said.

"*I* am the star of this show," she said haughtily.
"*I* am the star of this show," she said.

The second example in each set expresses the same tone and intent as the first, yet it does so without the extra adverb and, more important, without *leading* the reader. The reader is encouraged to infer the tone from the content of the writing.

Action Verbs Avoid the temptation to use action verbs as tags. Like adverbs tacked on to tags, they diminish the power of your dialogue. They are often redundant, and they tend to compete with the dialogue for the reader's attention. If the dialogue is well-written, action verbs aren't necessary, for the same reason that adding an adverb is not necessary: everything you need to know is in the dialogue itself. Consider this example:

> "Stop it!" she shouted.
>
> "Stop it!" she said.

The words, punctuation, and—if this sentence were part of a bigger scene—context tell us that the woman is probably shouting. There's no reason to insert "shouted" because it can be inferred.

If you want to suggest that a character delivers a line of dialogue in a specific way, consider writing a separate sentence. It will prevent redundancy and will also give you the chance to provide specific detail. Take a look at these two examples:

> "Stop it!" He shrieked like a school girl.
>
> His dad sighed in resignation. "Okay. You can take the car tonight."

Punctuate Correctly

Compelling dialogue, rich subtext, and clear dialogue tags are essential to creating an excellent short story. Just as important is knowing how to correctly punctuate your dialogue. It may seem like a nit-picky point, but correct punctuation will help your readers focus on your dialogue and keep them from getting distracted or confused. As you become more experienced as a writer, the seven basic rules that we provide for you here will become second nature.

1. Put all dialogue in quotation marks:

> "The view from here is beautiful."

2. When a quote is a complete sentence without attribution (a tag), you should insert a period *inside* the quotation marks at the end of the sentence:

> "The mountains are spectacular."

3. If a complete sentence is attributed to a speaker (i.e., if it has a dialogue tag), insert a comma *inside* the quotation marks and put a period after the dialogue tag. Remember that dialogue tags are *always* part of the sentence—they never stand alone:

> "The view from here is beautiful," he said.

4. If you want to put your dialogue tag in the middle of a sentence, put a comma inside the first set of closing quotation marks *and* after the dialogue tag:

> "Ever since this morning," he said, "my allergies have been driving me crazy."

5. If your quotation ends with a question mark or exclamation point, put it inside the quotation marks. Your dialogue tag will still be lower case and will end with a period:

> "Did you remember the bug spray?" she asked.

6. If you introduce the dialogue, insert a comma before the opening quotation marks and start the quotation with a capital letter:

> She asked, "Did you remember the bug spray?"

7. If your character is speaking and the dialogue goes on for more than one paragraph, don't use closing quotation marks. When the new paragraph begins, use opening quotation marks. Use closing quotation marks only when the character is finished speaking completely:

> . . . and they came upon the house. "I've never seen such a beautiful log cabin," Blair said. "When I was younger, I used to go to a cabin in the woods in New Hampshire and spend the holidays there with my family. We'd skate on the pond and wrap all our presents

out in the barn, just because it was fun to be so secretive. It was freezing cold at night, but no one cared.

"Actually, this cabin brings back another memory too: my first trip to Iceland. As I rode the bus from the airport into the city center, I saw a house literally in the middle of nowhere. It wasn't a log cabin, but it had the same dark look." They stared at the house a moment longer, then went inside.

Exceptions to the Rules   Many writers opt to use other formats for their dialogue. James Joyce, for example, sets dialogue off with a dash rather than with quotation marks. Take a look at this short passage from *Ulysses:*

He had spoken himself into boldness. Stephen, shielding the gaping wounds which the words had left in his heart, said very coldly:

–I am not thinking of the offence to my mother.

–Of what then? Buck Mulligan asked.

–Of the offence to me, Stephen answered.

Buck Mulligan swung round on his heel.

–O, an impossible person! he exclaimed.

In addition to this kind of formatting, some writers italicize their dialogue. Some don't set it off at all. As with most rules, the rules for punctuating dialogue are—to some extent—made to be broken. However, always remember that your job as a writer is to communicate as clearly as possible. Using proper dialogue format is one way to keep your writing clear.

Dialogue in Action Take a look at this scene from Ambrose Bierce's "An Occurrence at Owl Creek Bridge":

> "The Yanks are repairing the railroads," said the man, "and are getting ready for another advance. They have reached the Owl Creek bridge, put it in order and built a stockade on the north bank. The commandant has issued an order, which is posted everywhere, declaring that any civilian caught interfering with the railroad, its bridges, tunnels or trains will be summarily hanged. I saw the order."
>
> "How far is it to the Owl Creek bridge?" Farquhar asked.
>
> "About thirty miles."
>
> "Is there no force on this side the creek?"
>
> "Only a picket post half a mile out, on the railroad, and a single sentinel at this end of the bridge."
>
> "Suppose a man—a civilian and student of hanging—should elude the picket post and perhaps get the better of the sentinel," said Farquhar, smiling, "what could he accomplish?"
>
> The soldier reflected. "I was there a month ago," he replied. "I observed that the flood of last winter had lodged a great quantity of driftwood against the wooden pier at this end of the bridge. It is now dry and would burn like tow."

This scene of dialogue performs two functions. First, it tells us some things about Farquhar, the protagonist: Farquhar is a civilian who would like to play the role of soldier and help the Southern cause. This scene also provides valuable exposition, delivering the back story to Farquhar's dire circumstances. Bierce begins by introducing a soldier (who is really a Federal scout) to provide the setup for Farquhar's crime. We learn that the Federal Army is repairing the railroads and that anyone caught interfering with "its bridges, tunnels, or trains" will be hanged. Farquhar's comments hint at an interest in the bridge that is more than casual. In the second half of the scene, Bierce uses subtext to convey Farquhar's intentions. Farquhar asks the soldier, hypothetically, what "a student of hanging"—or someone who is willing to interfere with the bridge at his own peril, thus risking "learning" about hanging—could accomplish if he evades the guards at the bridge. The soldier's response incites Farquhar to action, as he suggests that the bridge could "burn like tow," or a pile of dry kindling.

Through this exchange and the narrative in previous sections, we learn that Farquhar is being hanged for trying to help the Southern cause. The beauty of the scene is that, without *telling* us what exactly transpired, Bierce uses the dialogue and its subtext as unspoken narrative to imply that Farquhar tried and failed to burn the Owl Creek bridge and will be hanged as a result.

Exercises

- Eavesdrop. Sit in a public place, or in a busy area of your house, and try to write down everything you hear people saying for fifteen minutes. Be sure to include the pauses, stammerings, and verbal tics. Then choose an interesting snippet and turn it into a scene of dialogue. Use proper dialogue format, such as quotation marks, tags, and punctuation, to create the scene. Remember to eliminate anything that doesn't propel the conversation forward.

- Write a short conversation between two characters and give each speaker a very distinctive verbal pattern, such as a tic, unique diction, or a habit. Then rewrite the same conversation, changing the characters' verbal patterns. Note how the tone, effect, and subtext of the conversation changes depending on *how* your characters speak.

- Write a short dialogue scene that communicates a conflict between two characters solely through subtext. Neither character in the scene should acknowledge or address the conflict directly.

Revision

Every writer loves the elation of typing out "The End" on the last page of a short story. After thinking so much about setting, plot, characters, beginnings, and endings, it's a relief to finally have something that feels complete. However, just because you've reached the end of your story doesn't mean you've reached the end of the writing process. A first draft is a huge accomplishment—but your story won't reach its full potential until you've gone back to revise it.

Revision is vital—it's not a step you should skip. Think of it this way: before you started writing, you spent a lot of time developing your story and figuring out important details. You should spend just as much time—maybe even more time—revising your story once the writing is finished. The attention you give your story during the revision process is just as important as the attention you give it during the planning and writing phases. You can learn how to revise skillfully to take your work to new heights. Some of your best writing is probably yet to come.

8

Give It Time

When you first complete a draft of a story, your mind is so full of it that it's nearly impossible to see the story for what it is. Some people see perfection, missing the obvious glitches and holes. Others see utter disaster and dramatically give up. Neither extreme will help you to revise your story in a way that will make it better. Instead of starting the revision process right away, you should wait—a day, a week, or however long you can go without forgetting about it or giving up.

If possible, set a date to return to the manuscript. When that date comes, read the story again, beginning to end. Read it once, just to get a sense of it and remind yourself what you wrote. Then read it a second time to actually start making changes. If you wait, we promise that you will see both strengths and weaknesses that you never would have seen otherwise. If you give it time, you'll see your story with new eyes, which is exactly what the word *revision* means: re-vision; seeing again.

Print It Out

If you've written your story on a computer, it's a good idea to print it out and mark up the pages by hand. Computers get us used to skimming—our eyes tend to just skate over material. The things we're used to reading on computer screens—websites, instant messages, pop-up ads, blogs, spam—don't really call for our complete attention. If you try to work with your story on the screen, you may wind up not reading it very carefully. Revision requires that you focus on every single word.

So print out your story, and use a pen or pencil to make your changes. This can make the process more definite. If a word or line works, it stays; if it doesn't work, it gets scribbled out. A paper copy also helps you to see the sweep of your story. When your story is on a computer screen, you can't get an impression of more than one page at a time. Having the entire story in your hands helps you get a sense of your story as a whole.

Think Big

Your first round of revisions should be global, meaning that you are reading for big issues. It's okay to be ruthless. This is the time to make big changes. Move or remove sections *boldly*. No matter how much you might love a particular line or paragraph, if it throws your story off or seems out of place, it must go. Sometimes you have to cut things that you like. But don't worry: if you wrote something that good once, you surely will again. And just because you cut it out of this story doesn't mean it has to disappear completely. Save it in a notebook or in a new document on your computer. You might decide to use it in another story in the future.

When you start revising, you should think about four main issues:

1. Unity
2. Voice
3. Character
4. Flow

Unity   First, try to confirm that your story makes sense. It should hold together and feel like it's all of one piece. Check consistency. Plot elements may change as you write, so make sure that if it's a jade monkey the archeologists in your story are after, your first paragraph doesn't refer to a monkey made of solid bronze. Consistency covers more than just plot.

Check your tone and your mood and make sure they don't wildly shift from paragraph to paragraph. Novels can afford to ramble in places, but a short story needs to be tight.

Voice Sometimes the voice in your story can change as you get more comfortable with it and get to know it better. Check to make sure the voice is consistent, especially in the beginning of the story. If the early paragraphs seem like they came from an entirely different story, you may have to rework them. Also, as the climax of your story approaches, make sure the voice stays steady—don't let your librarian start sounding like an action hero. Make sure your narrator stays in character no matter what the situation.

Character Writers kill off characters all the time. When you revise your story, ask yourself if each character serves a purpose. If you find that two of your characters are pretty much the same, you have a few options: one needs to go completely, one or both require significant alteration, or they need to be blended into one character. Each character must pull his or her own weight—or else you must find a way to say good-bye.

Flow Flow is an elusive quality that describes the way your story "reads." That is, reading your story should be a pleasant experience for your readers. Flow means that the parts of your story fit together and that scenes connect clearly. Readers shouldn't be confused about why things are happening when, or who's doing them. When you revise, make sure that your story isn't too choppy and that the transitions between scenes are clear and logical. Endings are especially important for flow: the ending should feel like an ending. The last lines should have some resonance. Otherwise, you may leave your readers feeling like they're missing a page. You may have to add some material in order to improve the flow of your story.

Know the Pitfalls

When you're making the big changes to your story, you should keep your eyes open for some of the problems that often plague short stories. If you do find one or more of these problems, don't worry. Even the best short story writers fall into these traps. Flaws are rarely fatal in short stories—this is what revision is for. Some of the most common pitfalls are the following:

- Banality
- Lack of tension
- Shortcuts to tension
- Talking down to readers
- Clichés

Banality   A story needs a reason to be. If it just relates some things that happened, or just recounts some scenes from ordinary life, readers won't be very interested. It's not that ordinary life doesn't have a place in short fiction—it's the foundation of many great short stories. But ordinary life isn't enough *on its own* to justify a reader's commitment to your work. There must be a story that goes beyond the banality, that reveals a glimpse inside or beyond it, that tells us something about it that moves or surprises us. In other words, a short story has to be a little *extra*-ordinary. The language you use in your story must also be more ambitious than what we might read in the average, everyday blog. Otherwise, we'd just read blogs and not bother with stories. For example, while in a blog you might dash off "The beach at Cape Cod was awesome," you'll want to be more thoughtful about your description when you write a short story.

Lack of Tension   When you reread your story in the revision process, make sure that there are sources of tension pulsing in the background. Without conflict, a story is flat and static. Your characters should have goals and motivation. Without the tension that accompanies a character's drive, your story won't really go anywhere. A short story demands tension; otherwise, it just falls apart. Remember: readers should want to know what will happen; they should want to read on. If they don't, you've probably written a sketch or an exercise, not a story.

Shortcuts to Tension   When you're writing a first draft, you may get buried in language and dialogue and forget to build up tension based on conflict and dilemma. You may then try to overcompensate by trying to hide the missing tension under big, loud scenes—shortcuts to tension. Gratuitous sex and violence are common shortcuts, as is an overabundance of expletives. By including these shortcuts, you're not adding something valuable to the story—you're trying to distract readers from realizing what your story is missing.

This is not to say that sex, cursing, and gunplay don't have a place in short fiction. They certainly can work effectively. Just make sure that if you include them, they complement the tension in your story rather than replace it.

Talking Down to Readers Writers are professional communicators—and they don't want to be misunderstood. But talking down to your readers isn't the way to get them to engage with your story. When you revise, think about how you're coming across to your readers. If you've said something once, they'll probably get it; there's no need to pound them over the head with it. Readers are also pretty good about catching symbolism, even if it's subtle or unusual. If you want to foreshadow a death, you'll probably want to come up with something more subtle than a skull in a cupboard—such obvious symbolism suggests that you don't think your readers are intelligent enough to understand you. Likewise, if you have a lesson or a moral that you want to get across, try not to be too obvious. Forcing your readers to wade through preachy paragraph after preachy paragraph will make them feel condescended to and will lessen the impact of your story.

Clichés Finding and eliminating clichés may prove to be one of your hardest tasks during the revision process. To make your work fresh, you have to carefully envision each and every scene, gesture, comment, and character—this is the only way to make them original. We all fall into the cliché trap. Some clichés are catchphrases that may sneak into your text, perhaps taking the form of dialogue that doesn't sound much like the way real people talk: "Search me. I'm an open book." Other clichés are scenarios. Does every writer have to sit over a typewriter, his forehead in his hands, with balls of crumbled paper scattered all around him? Does every hooker have a heart of gold? Stereotypes like these can quickly deaden a story, and they suggest that you have not spent much time thinking about your work. When you catch a cliché in your own short story, eliminate it and replace it with something more original.

Consider Verb Tense

During your revision you should review your choice of tense. Tense refers to verbs and whether the story's action took place in the past, takes place in the present, or will take place in the future. Ask yourself if the tense you've chosen is the best for your material. Try switching it to see if you like the effect of another tense better. If you have a narrator who's wiser than the events he or she describes, you may be better off with the past tense. If you have an action story that's fueled by pure adrenaline, present tense is probably your best bet. Also confirm that your tense is consistent. Few things are as distracting to readers as unexplained shifts between tenses. There are four tenses you can choose from:

- Past tense
- Present tense
- Future tense
- Mixed tense

You made a choice when you wrote your first draft, even if it was an unconscious choice. When you revise, you should consider whether you made the right choice. Changing verb tense is common—and it can be the key that unlocks your story's success. Take a look at the following descriptions of each tense to determine which makes sense for your story.

Past Tense   In past tense, the narrator is looking backward. Events are being recalled some time after they occurred. Sometimes writers will explain where and when they're recording what happened, but this is definitely optional. Past tense is easy to read. It also tends to induce fewer questions in readers, so it's the most readily believable tense. Here's what past tense looks like:

> They shimmied and shook as they whirled around the dance floor.

Present Tense   Modern short stories frequently use the present tense. In the present tense, events in the story are happening right now, in real time. The advantage of present tense is that it moves quickly and comes with its own natural urgency. The disadvantage is that it can be less believable— readers may be asking themselves how the author is managing to write all this down. Present tense looks like this:

> They shimmy and shake as they whirl around the dance floor.

Future Tense   Future tense is rarely used. It's the tense where things are going to happen. It's a little awkward, and it's not very believable (it's hard for a writer to convey much authority about things that haven't even happened yet), which accounts for its rarity. The future tense looks like this:

They will shimmy and shake as they whirl around the dance floor.

Mixed Tense   Mixed tenses can be tricky to use. Readers get used to a fictional universe with a particular viewpoint, and it's jarring to see that viewpoint change. Generally, mixed tenses work best when there is only a brief switch to an alternative tense. Our model story, "An Occurrence at Owl Creek Bridge," uses mixed tense skillfully. The entire story is written in the past tense, except for the second-to-last paragraph, which is written in present tense. The final sentence returns to the past tense. (See The Short Story in Action, page 169, for the complete short story.) The effect of the abrupt return is dramatic: all the false hope that was expressed during the present tense passage is suddenly slammed by the main character's demise. This limited use of a mixed tense greatly enhances the impact of the story's end.

Think Small

After you've done the heavy-lifting part of revising your story, you should narrow your focus from global to local. Instead of working on large chunks or aspects of your story, you'll now focus on individual scenes, paragraphs, and sentences. You can be just as ruthless here as you were in your global edit—but this time you'll be wiping out a few words with the stroke of your pen, not long passages or entire characters. There are three main elements to consider when you do revision on a smaller scale:

1. Specifics
2. Repetition
3. Rhythm

Specifics   Check over your nouns and adjectives to make sure they're accurate and specific. Ask yourself how well you can see your setting. If it's vague, you may need to add another sentence or two to fill in the visuals. Do the same with your characters. If they're not popping off the page, they may need another line of description or more reinforcement of a character trait.

Repetition   In a short story, there isn't room for any flab, so you should eliminate as much repetition as possible. Repetition occurs frequently when you use adjectives. In general, one adjective is enough—including too many may create redundancy. For example, if a character has swollen feet one morning, you don't need to also say that his feet are puffy, bulging, and chubby. Don't use three words where one will suffice, and strive to make your writing as simple and clear as possible.

Rhythm   Rhythm is one of the most underrated elements of good writing. To evaluate rhythm in your story, read all or part of it out loud to yourself. Listen to the flow of words and to the cadence of your sentences. If your prose sounds choppy, smooth it out. Try making sentences shorter. Try making them longer. If a word sticks out like a sore thumb, substitute a synonym. A story may also sound clumsy in places where sentence structure doesn't vary. If you catch four sentences in a row that begin "She was . . . ," you'll probably want to make some revisions.

Revising Rhythm in Action   There is not one surefire way to improve the rhythm of your story. It usually takes some experimentation to find what works and sounds best. Take a look at this sentence with a standard order of "subject followed by a verb":

He was going back to the gym when he saw the car, a red Mazda.

This is the most common way of stating information, but it's not the only way, and using it too frequently creates a dull rhythm. When you revise, consider how you can change the order of your sentences to improve rhythm. You could put the preposition in front:

On his way back to the gym he saw the car. It was a red Mazda.

You can change the emphasis of your sentence by changing the subject. Here, we emphasize the car rather than the "he":

A red Mazda was what he saw on his way back to the gym.

You can also vary sentence structure by adjusting the length. Try merging two sentences into one long one. Or make them very short, like the following:

He was going back to the gym. He saw the car. A red Mazda.

Working closely with your prose this way is a vital part of the revision process. It can mean the difference between a so-so story and a stunning one. Keep in mind that you don't have to use the same rhythm the whole way through; in fact, doing so may make your story sound repetitive. Think of rhythm as a tool you can use to call attention to certain ideas and scenes. Changing the rhythm can create dramatic effect and can affect the atmosphere and tone of your story.

Think Really Small

The final step in the revision process is to examine your story on a micro level, word by word. Look one last time for excess; trim wherever you can. Some writers make their final read by going backward, line by line. This way you pay attention to individual words and lines, without being distracted by the story. In your final round of revisions, check the following:

- Adjectives are used sparingly.
- Adverbs are used sparingly.
- Passive voice is used sparingly.
- Every line of dialogue serves some purpose.
- Who's speaking in the dialogue is easy to determine.
- Sentences aren't too wordy and difficult to read.
- Characters' names aren't used too often, particularly when pronouns would suffice.

Typos   Minor spelling errors and grammatical mistakes may seem unimportant, since your story will be clear regardless. However, if you take your work seriously, you'll want others to do the same. Any mistake that sneaks through is going to distract the reader and interrupt what the writer John Gardner describes as the "fictional dream." A typo in your story is like a big piece of dust on a photograph—it distracts from the work. Before you consider a short story done, make sure it's as clean as it can possibly be.

Stop! Don't Over-Revise

Though it may sometimes seem like the revision process can go on forever, it does have an end. Think of your first draft as an overgrown tree. As you revise, you trim it into shape. Once it's in shape, however, continued clipping may damage the main branches that the tree needs to live. The moral of this metaphor? Don't over-revise. Make sure the core of your story stays intact no matter what. And when you feel you've done a thorough revision, put the story aside and move on. Or at least put it aside for a day or two to regain some perspective.

Revision in Action   Take a look at the first draft of the opening to a short story about a man trying to wriggle out of a lawsuit:

> Will was adamant about not wanting a lawyer. Lawyers cost money, lots of money, and Will refused to spend it. And in any case, he was sure the charges were unwarranted. A judge was just going

to throw the case out anyway, so what was the point in dropping big sums of cash on unnecessary legal accessories?

A defiant look hardened on Will's face as he thought about it. It was an old-fashioned face, Will's, like the faces people had a long time ago. There was something dark in it, too, some distant damage. A quick glance at his preppy clothes suggested WASP America, though if you looked longer you'd realize that the clothes had frays at their ends and his shoes were worn. He wouldn't shave for days on end. He'd moved around a lot as a kid, so it wasn't totally surprising that he looked the way he did.

"Hey, how are you?" I asked, as I met him in the little uptown bar we used to prefer for hanging out. It was quiet and subdued, and hence perfect for conversation.

"I'm doing alright," Will answered. "How about yourself?"

"Can't complain. Now what's all this I hear about you looking for a lawyer?"

"I don't need a lawyer. It's not going to come to that. The judge will dismiss it in five seconds. He'll laugh Suzy Powell and her supposed defamation suit right out of the courtroom."

"I don't think you should take chances with something as potentially serious as a lawsuit," I said.

Look closely at this first draft—it has a lot of problems. There is some throat-clearing at the beginning. The writer is trying to lay out the scene, but he does it in a clumsy way. The opening isn't very gripping, and it's loaded with repetition. A similar excess of exposition appears in the dialogue. It's realistic, for the most part, but it doesn't illustrate much beyond the fact that the two characters know each other.

Within the small confines of a short story, there just isn't room for this much warming up. Here's what the revision might look like:

> "I don't need a lawyer. It's not going to come to that. The judge will dismiss it in five seconds. He'll laugh Suzy Powell and her supposed defamation suit right out of the courtroom."
>
> Defiance hardens on Will's face. It's a nineteen-forties face, Will's, all-American and friendly, but with something vaguely damaged there, too, as if he'd seen a little too much overseas. A quick glance at his preppy clothes might suggest six post-Mayflower generations. A longer look reveals thrift shop provenance in his frayed cuffs, the stained tongues of his shoes. As the son of an electrical engineer who never stayed in the same job, or town, for more than a year, the haphazard look was probably inevitable. It doesn't help that Will won't buy razors because he considers them more of the superfluous offal our society is drowning in. The perennial growth of beard on his cheeks only intensifies the effect of good-stock-gone-to-seed.
>
> "That's pure hubris," I said. "Cheapskate: *get a lawyer.*"

There's a big difference between the first version and the revision. Take a look at where we made the heavy cuts:

> ~~Will was adamant about not wanting a lawyer. Lawyers cost money, lots of money, and Will refused to spend it. And in any case, he was sure the charges were unwarranted. A judge was just going to throw the case out anyway, so what was the point in dropping big sums of cash on unnecessary legal accessories?~~

~~A defiant look hardened on Will's face as he thought about~~ ~~it.~~ It was an old-fashioned face, Will's, like the faces people had a long time ago. There was something dark in it, too, some distant damage. A quick glance at his preppy clothes suggested WASP America, though if you looked longer you'd realize that the clothes had frays at their ends and his shoes were worn. He wouldn't shave for days on end. He'd moved around a lot as a kid, so it wasn't totally surprising that he looked the way he did.

~~"Hey, how are you?" I asked, as I met him in the little uptown~~ ~~bar we used to prefer for hanging out. It was quiet and subdued, and~~ ~~hence perfect for conversation.~~

~~"I'm doing alright," Will answered. "How about yourself?"~~

~~"Can't complain. Now what's all this I hear about you looking for~~ ~~a lawyer?"~~

"I don't need a lawyer. It's not going to come to that. The judge will dismiss it in five seconds. He'll laugh Suzy Powell and her supposed defamation right out of the courtroom."

~~"I don't think you should take chances with something as~~ ~~potentially serious as a lawsuit," I said.~~

In the revision, we replaced the ponderous lead with an *in medias res* introduction that we moved up from the dialogue section. It's more mysterious and more likely to be intriguing. Notice that we changed the verb tense in the revision. The first draft used past tense, but the revision uses present. The story moves more quickly now.

You'll also notice the details have become more specific. The first draft described Will's face as the kind people had "a long time ago." That vague and boring assessment now reads "a nineteen-forties face." We may not be entirely sure what the writer meant by that, but there's definitely more for us to draw an impression from. "The clothes had frays at their ends and his shoes were worn" has become "a longer look reveals thrift shop provenance in his frayed cuffs, the stained tongues of his shoes." The phrase "stained tongues" has a nice ring to it, subtlety reinforcing the portrait of a cheap, neglectful individual. The writer has also set aside space to explain the origins of this trait: "He'd moved around a lot as a kid" has been upgraded to "the son of an electrical engineer who never stayed in the same job, or town, for more than a year."

One other key change to note is in the narrator's dialogue. Look at the difference between these two versions:

FIRST DRAFT: "I don't think you should take chances with something as potentially serious as a lawsuit," I said.

REVISION: "That's pure hubris," I said. "Cheapskate: *get a lawyer.*"

Changing just this one statement alters our impression of the narrator. In the first draft, he seemed stiff and buttoned-up. In the revision we get the sense that he's blunt and not afraid to stand up to his friend. He may be pompous: he's not embarrassed to throw around a word like *hubris*. The new line is a lot less generic than the original, allowing readers to form more of a picture of the speaker. As an added bonus, the new dialogue takes up less space than the original. Trying to say more with less, as the author did here in going from the 255 words to 166 words, is one of the great challenges of writing short fiction.

Exercises

- Find a sample of fiction you don't like and try editing it into a shape that you do like and can call your own. This is good practice for making radical cuts. You'll also get an idea of what it's like to justify the existence of every line and word in a piece.

- Isolate a descriptive section from one of your own short stories or from a published story. Try to expand it. Ask yourself what details you or the writer may have overlooked. See how layered you can make the description without resorting to repetition.

- Take one of your own short stories or a published story. Through cuts and edits, try to get it down to 500 words. Then 250 words. Then 50. Does it still work? How much is it diminished in comparison to its original version? This exercise will help you see what's most essential in a piece.

Writing Workshops

When you work on a story for a long time, you can lose the ability to see it objectively: you're so familiar with it that it's more difficult to recognize weaknesses or problems. You're too in love with your story to actively critique its problems—like being unable to criticize or see any faults in your latest, most fabulous girlfriend or boyfriend. Other people, however, have never seen your story before—they can look at it with fresh eyes and point out things that you may have never seen on your own. One way to have others see your work on a regular basis is to form a writing workshop.

9

Getting feedback on your work makes your stories better—but it can help your writing in another way too. By reading other people's work closely and making thoughtful comments, you'll gain a deeper understanding of story writing in general. You'll be more finely attuned to how fiction-writing techniques work in real stories, and you'll be able to apply what you learn to your own writing.

Be Open to Critique

You can't predict what people are going to say about your story, and you may find yourself facing a bewildering array of comments. Some people will love it. Some may hate it. Some will think it's too long, while others will want ten more pages. Remember that you've written a story for other people to read—be prepared for the reality that people will have varying opinions of your work.

When facing these opinions in a workshop, simply write them down and digest them later. Don't try to argue, disagree, or defend. These are *opinions* of your story—people are entitled to have them. This is your chance to find out what people think. In the end, the only person you have to please is yourself.

Set Up an Effective Workshop

A workshop is a collective of writers who come together to discuss their work. However, the most important aspect of a writing workshop is that it gives you critical feedback to help you *improve* your stories. Over the years, professional and student writers have come to a few conclusions about what makes a workshop effective. You should consider these elements when you're thinking about starting your own workshop.

Location   Location often has a direct impact on a workshop's success; it sets the tone and atmosphere for the workshop. Location can also affect how productive you are as a group. A lively atmosphere might *seem* ideal, but if the location is too crowded and noisy, you may find it too distracting to get much accomplished. On the other hand, environments like the library and empty classrooms can seem so impersonal and academic that you may start to dread going to the workshop. Ideal locations are convenient to reach, comfortable, and quiet enough to encourage focus. Consider having workshop members take turns hosting the meeting at their homes. If there are four or more people in the workshop, each member will have to host only once a month for a weekly workshop. A local coffee shop during off-peak hours can be a quiet and comfortable alternative.

Size   Think small—but not too small. The ideal size for a workshop is somewhere between four and seven people. Truth be told, there will almost always be people who can't make a meeting for one reason or another, so your group should be big enough to absorb an absence or two and still offer writers feedback from multiple people. At the same time, a large group—with, say, more than six or seven people—can be cumbersome. Staying focused, finding large enough locations, and making sure that everyone has an opportunity to present their work become more difficult in a large group. You also run the risk of feedback overload— receiving so many comments on a story that it becomes difficult to incorporate them into your work.

Participants   Resist the urge to fill your workshop with friends that have only a casual interest in writing. You'll benefit most from your workshop if it is reserved for people who are serious about writing and want real, constructive criticism. If you have friends who are committed to writing and can commit to the workshop, great. Otherwise, school message boards, English classes, and nearby college or university bulletin boards might be good places to seek out interested, serious writers. Age doesn't matter; a group of your peers can be good, but a mixed age group can be good as well. It all depends on who you find.

When you talk to prospective participants, try to gauge their interest level and their commitment to writing. Ask what they want to get out of a workshop and if they can commit to both the workshop meetings and the reading and writing in between. Remember, it doesn't really matter that you have great writers in the workshop; what matters is that the participants can attend consistently and provide thoughtful, constructive feedback.

Follow a Schedule

The best way to maintain order in a group of people eager to talk about their stories is to follow a schedule. Try to meet once a week, for a reasonable amount of time. Each person should have a turn without feeling short-changed by the dwindling attention of the group. The number of participants in your workshop will ultimately determine the workshop's length, but a good rule of thumb is that 2½ hours is the maximum time you can expect people to stay focused.

Set a specific limit on the time each participant's work is discussed. Otherwise, some people will get hours of discussion while others get only five minutes. Each person should have their work discussed for about 20–30 minutes. You should set an agenda before each meeting so that everyone knows who's work is going to be discussed and when. Controlling the meeting will ensure that each person accomplishes something.

Be Prepared

Make sure that everyone's work is sent out to all the participants before your workshop meets. Reading work during meetings is a waste of time, and participants won't have time to consider their feedback carefully. It's also a good idea to ask all the participants to print out the stories and write their comments on the pages. This way, you'll receive feedback from everyone, and you can read over the comments again on your own time.

Give Constructive Feedback

Constructive criticism is feedback that focuses on potential solutions rather than problems. It's the best way to help people to understand how to progress and make changes. You should never make fun of someone's story or writing style, and you shouldn't spend the entire time pointing out a story's flaws and problems. Constructive criticism is a way of *helping* someone out by pointing out possible flaws and offering suggestions on how to make the story better.

Helpful Hints Here are a few helpful hints for providing constructive criticism:

- Balance your comments. Just saying, "I like it" isn't much help, and a full-on critical attack is never acceptable. Try to say a few good things about the work (even if you really have to get creative), and offer a few suggestions for improvement. Never bully the other writer by just giving a list of things that you feel have to be changed.

- Don't tune out when you're not talking and the work being discussed is not yours. You'll be surprised what you can learn by listening to comments on another person's piece. You might find a solution or an idea you can use for your own work.

- Don't take things personally, and don't make the comments personal. If someone thinks your story needs some development, they aren't saying there is something wrong with you. Likewise, don't say things like, "Well, you know how you always talk too much about yourself? Well, your narrator does it too." Feelings can be easily hurt in workshops, so be conscious of the way you phrase your comments.

- There are usually a few very vocal people in every group, and one or two "I like it" people. Consider having a workshop moderator who can orchestrate the conversation—preventing the bullies from taking over, drawing the under-commentators out of the shadows, and making sure that everyone gets an equal amount of time.

- When someone is commenting on your work, don't comment back unless you are asked to give clarification. It can be hard, but sit back, listen, and take notes.

- Keep your emotions in check. It's a writing workshop, not a therapy session. Be honest, say what you feel, but remember that you are there for the **writing**. Polite, professional behavior is the way to go.

- Remember: you don't have to do what your workshop group suggests. In the end, the work is yours. It's up to you to select the comments you feel are most useful.

Constructive Praise   Constructive praise doesn't mean throwing flowers at a story. It's good to offer well-deserved compliments to the writer, but don't limit your comments to positive reinforcement. The workshop exists to place the writer's *work* under a critical lens. When praising a writer's work, try to avoid generalities ("I just loved the whole thing"). Praise is best offered in specifics: "The dialogue was really funny, and I liked how it established the underlying tension between the protagonist and his sister."

Learn to Read Critically

Reading for pleasure and reading critically involve two very different sets of skills. The latter involves casting an analytical eye on every line. As a workshop reader, your goal is to identify inconsistencies, gaps, and other problems in the story and then suggest possible solutions. You may not have time to read the story twice, so it's vital to analyze multiple elements of the story at once: structure, character development, voice, dialogue, etc. Unless the piece is very, very short, resist the urge to read it in one sitting. Read a few pages at a time, slowly and attentively, and note your observations in the margin or on a separate piece of paper.

Don't procrastinate. That will lead you to rush your reading, and your feedback will suffer as a result. The best approach is to treat others' work as you want your own to be treated.

What to Look For   It's helpful to know what to look for as your read someone else's story. As you read others' work, ask yourself the questions in the following list. You may find it helpful to copy this list and hand it out to everyone in the workshop—it will encourage valuable feedback.

- Is the title effective? Does it reflect the story's theme or plot in any way?

- Does the beginning draw you in? Does it effectively set the scene for the story? Why or why not?

- Does the author establish the characters and setting with vivid description?

- Does the writer make good use of metaphor, simile, imagery, or other literary devices to help tell the story?

- Does the prose have a sense of rhythm? Does it flow naturally?

- Is the narration clear and consistent? Does the narrator's tone serve the story well?

- Does the author paint vivid characters? Can you see them clearly as you read the story?

- Does every character have a clear purpose in the story? Does each character have a role in propelling the story forward?

- Is there discernable conflict between the protagonist and the antagonist?

- Is the dialogue compelling? Does it ring true? Does it propel the story forward in some way?

- What happens during the story to change the protagonist? Does the protagonist change?

- What is the story lacking? What does the story need less of?

- Does the story seem carefully written?

- Is the story's ending effective? Why or why not?

- Do you feel the story is affecting or revealing in some way? Why or why not?

- How do you feel after reading the story?

Accept Feedback Gracefully

Reading others' work critically and providing constructive criticism is difficult; even more difficult is sitting quietly while your own work is being discussed. Receiving comments on your work can be difficult for three main reasons:

- It's hard to keep up with everyone's comments, especially when they contradict one another.
- You have to think quickly to process the information you're given and figure out if it works or not.
- You have to deal with people tearing apart your precious writing—people who may have never heard of constructive criticism.

To deal with feedback gracefully, stay organized. Bring a copy of your story and a notebook to the workshop. Try to write down every comment or note you get so you can remember them when you leave. Make sure you understand each comment; ask for clarification if you're confused. Don't worry about seeming dense—you won't be able to implement a great comment if you don't understand it.

One important guideline: try not to argue with people who are volunteering constructive criticism. You'll probably get feedback you disagree with, but don't pick a fight. It's up to you what comments to listen to. If you think something is off base, note it down then move on.

Keeping Perspective   Remember: a workshop isn't there to write a story for you. In the end, it's your story.

Think about what others have said, and think about your strengths and weaknesses in general. If you're sure about something, but no one else is, there's nothing wrong with doing it your way.

Submit Your Work

Once you've subjected your story to others' comments and made a final round of revisions, what's next? Do you put your story on a shelf somewhere? Of course not. Stories are meant to be read by others—and not just your friends and family. Once your story is in top form, consider submitting it to magazines, newspapers, or websites for publication. There are many print and electronic venues targeted at a young audience who publish submissions from their readers. Your inner critic may resist the idea ("My stuff is not good enough"), but you shouldn't listen. All published writers were once like you: not published. One day they sent in a story, an editor liked it, and from that day forward they were published writers. There's no reason why that can't happen to you.

Guidelines Every magazine or website has guidelines for submitting short fiction. To have your story considered for publication, look for the "How to Submit" or "Submission Guidelines" section. The guidelines will tell you exactly how to submit your story, and you should follow them exactly. Literary magazines receive many submissions each week, and one way to weed out writers is to disqualify those who have not followed the submission guidelines. Give your story the best possible chance of being accepted by making sure it meets all requirements for length, format, and, in some cases, subject matter.

The Short Story in Action

Throughout this book, we've shown you how character development, dialogue, description, and other elements of story-writing play out in Ambrose Bierce's short story "An Occurrence at Owl Creek Bridge." What follows is the complete short story. Bierce knew well the military setting he evokes—he actually fought for the Union army during the Civil War. Although the story was written in 1886, it still has cultural currency, even making a recent appearance on an episode of the television show *Lost*. The character John Locke, while organizing a bookshelf, examined a copy of "An Occurrence at Owl Creek Bridge." The inclusion of the story reinforced some viewers' suspicions that the events on the island were really just the dreams of doomed characters, just as the events in the story are only fantasies of the main character, Farquhar.

10

"An Occurrence at Owl Creek Bridge" by Ambrose Bierce

I

A man stood upon a railroad bridge in northern Alabama, looking down into the swift water twenty feet below. The man's hands were behind his back, the wrists bound with a cord. A rope closely encircled his neck. It was attached to a stout cross-timber above his head and the slack fell to the level of his knees. Some loose boards laid upon the sleepers supporting the metals of the railway supplied a footing for him and his executioners—two private soldiers of the Federal army, directed by a sergeant who in civil life may have been a deputy sheriff. At a short remove upon the same temporary platform was an officer in the uniform of his rank, armed. He was a captain. A sentinel at each end of the bridge stood with his rifle in the position known as "support," that is to say, vertical in front of the left shoulder, the hammer resting on the forearm thrown straight across the chest—a formal and unnatural position, enforcing an erect carriage of the body. It did not appear to be the duty of these two men to know what was occurring at the center of the bridge; they merely blockaded the two ends of the foot planking that traversed it.

Beyond one of the sentinels nobody was in sight; the railroad ran straight away into a forest for a hundred yards, then, curving, was lost to view. Doubtless there was an outpost farther along. The other bank of the stream was open ground—a gentle acclivity topped with a stockade of vertical tree trunks, loopholed for rifles, with a single embrasure through which protruded the muzzle of a brass cannon commanding the bridge. Midway of the slope between the bridge and fort were the spectators—a single company of infantry in line, at "parade rest," the butts of the rifles on the ground, the barrels inclining slightly backward against the right shoulder, the hands crossed upon the stock. A lieutenant stood at the right of the line, the point of his sword upon the ground, his left hand resting upon his right. Excepting the group of four at the center of the bridge, not a man moved. The company faced the bridge, staring stonily, motionless. The sentinels, facing the banks of the stream, might have been statues to adorn the bridge. The captain stood with folded arms, silent, observing the work of his subordinates, but making no sign. Death is a dignitary who when he comes announced is to be received with formal manifestations of respect, even by those most familiar with him. In the code of military etiquette silence and fixity are forms of deference.

The man who was engaged in being hanged was apparently about thirty-five years of age. He was a civilian, if one might judge from his habit, which was that of a planter. His features were good—a straight nose, firm mouth, broad forehead, from which his long, dark hair was combed straight back, falling behind his ears to the collar of his well-fitting frock coat. He wore a mustache and pointed beard, but no whiskers; his eyes were large and dark gray, and had a kindly expression which one would hardly have expected in one whose neck was in the hemp. Evidently this was no vulgar assassin. The liberal military code makes provision for hanging many kinds of persons, and gentlemen are not excluded.

The preparations being complete, the two private soldiers stepped aside and each drew away the plank upon which he had been standing. The sergeant turned to the captain, saluted and placed himself immediately behind that officer, who in turn moved apart one pace. These movements left the condemned man and the sergeant standing on the two ends of the same plank, which spanned three of the cross-ties of the bridge. The end upon which the civilian stood almost, but not quite, reached a fourth. This plank had been held in place by the weight of the captain; it was now held by that of the sergeant. At a signal from the former the latter would step aside, the plank would tilt and the condemned man go down between two ties. The arrangement commended itself to his judgment as simple and effective. His face had not been covered nor his eyes bandaged. He looked a moment at his "unsteadfast footing," then let his gaze wander to the swirling water of the stream racing madly beneath his feet. A piece of dancing driftwood caught his attention and his eyes followed it down the current. How slowly it appeared to move! What a sluggish stream!

He closed his eyes in order to fix his last thoughts upon his wife and children. The water, touched to gold by the early sun, the brooding mists under the banks at some distance down the stream, the fort, the soldiers, the piece of drift—all had distracted him. And now he became conscious of a new disturbance. Striking through the thought of his dear ones was a sound which he could neither ignore nor understand, a sharp, distinct, metallic percussion like the stroke of a blacksmith's hammer upon the anvil; it had the same ringing quality. He wondered what it was, and whether immeasurably distant or near by—it seemed both. Its recurrence was regular, but as slow as the tolling of a death knell. He awaited each stroke with impatience and—he knew not why—apprehension. The intervals of silence grew progressively longer, the delays became maddening. With their greater infrequency the sounds increased in strength and sharpness. They hurt his ear like the thrust of a knife; he feared he would shriek. What he heard was the ticking of his watch.

He unclosed his eyes and saw again the water below him. "If I could free my hands," he thought, "I might throw off the noose and spring into the stream. By diving I could evade the bullets and, swimming vigorously, reach the bank, take to the woods and get away home. My home, thank God, is as yet outside their lines; my wife and little ones are still beyond the invader's farthest advance."

As these thoughts, which have here to be set down in words, were flashed into the doomed man's brain rather than evolved from it the captain nodded to the sergeant. The sergeant stepped aside.

II

Peyton Farquhar was a well-to-do planter, of an old and highly respected Alabama family. Being a slave owner and like other slave owners a politician he was naturally an original secessionist and ardently devoted to the Southern cause. Circumstances of an imperious nature, which it is unnecessary to relate here, had prevented him from taking service with the gallant army that had fought the disastrous campaigns ending with the fall of Corinth, and he chafed under the inglorious restraint, longing for the release of his energies, the larger life of the soldier, the opportunity for distinction. That opportunity, he felt, would come, as it comes to all in war time. Meanwhile he did what he could. No service was too humble for him to perform in aid of the South, no adventure too perilous for him to undertake if consistent with the character of a civilian who was at heart a soldier, and who in good faith and without too much qualification assented to at least a part of the frankly villainous dictum that all is fair in love and war.

One evening while Farquhar and his wife were sitting on a rustic bench near the entrance to his grounds, a gray-clad soldier rode up to the gate and asked for a drink of water. Mrs. Farquhar was only too happy to serve him with her own white hands. While she was fetching the water her husband approached the dusty horseman and inquired eagerly for news from the front.

"The Yanks are repairing the railroads," said the man, "and are getting ready for another advance. They have reached the Owl Creek bridge, put it in order and built a stockade on the north bank. The commandant has issued an order, which is posted everywhere, declaring that any civilian caught interfering with the railroad, its bridges, tunnels or trains will be summarily hanged. I saw the order."

"How far is it to the Owl Creek bridge?" Farquhar asked.

"About thirty miles."

"Is there no force on this side the creek?"

"Only a picket post half a mile out, on the railroad, and a single sentinel at this end of the bridge."

"Suppose a man–a civilian and student of hanging–should elude the picket post and perhaps get the better of the sentinel," said Farquhar, smiling, "what could he accomplish?"

The soldier reflected. "I was there a month ago," he replied. "I observed that the flood of last winter had lodged a great quantity of driftwood against the wooden pier at this end of the bridge. It is now dry and would burn like tow."

The lady had now brought the water, which the soldier drank. He thanked her ceremoniously, bowed to her husband and rode away. An hour later, after nightfall, he repassed the plantation, going northward in the direction from which he had come. He was a Federal scout.

III

As Peyton Farquhar fell straight downward through the bridge he lost consciousness and was as one already dead. From this state he was awakened–ages later, it seemed to him–by the pain of a sharp pressure upon his throat, followed by a sense of suffocation. Keen, poignant agonies seemed to shoot from his neck downward through every fiber of his body and limbs. These pains appeared to flash along well-defined lines of ramification and to beat with an inconceivably rapid periodicity. They seemed like streams of pulsating fire heating him to an intolerable temperature. As to his head, he was conscious of nothing but a feeling of fullness–of congestion. These sensations were unaccompanied by thought. The intellectual part of his nature was already effaced; he had power only to feel, and feeling was torment. He was conscious of motion. Encompassed in a luminous cloud, of which he was now merely the fiery heart, without material substance, he swung through unthinkable arcs of oscillation, like a vast pendulum. Then all at once, with terrible suddenness, the light about him shot upward with the noise of a loud splash; a frightful roaring was in his ears, and all was cold and dark. The power of thought was restored; he knew that the rope had broken and he had fallen into the stream. There was no additional strangulation; the noose about his neck was already suffocating him and kept the water from his lungs. To die of hanging at the bottom of a river!–the idea seemed to him ludicrous. He opened his eyes in the darkness and saw above him a gleam of light, but how distant, how inaccessible! He was still sinking, for the light became fainter and fainter until it was a mere glimmer. Then it began to grow and brighten, and he knew that he was rising toward the surface–knew it with reluctance, for he was now very comfortable. "To be hanged and drowned," he thought? "that is not so bad; but I do not wish to be shot. No; I will not be shot; that is not fair."

He was not conscious of an effort, but a sharp pain in his wrist apprised him that he was trying to free his hands. He gave the struggle his attention, as an idler might observe the feat of a juggler, without interest in the outcome. What splendid effort!– what magnificent, what superhuman strength! Ah, that was a fine endeavor! Bravo! The cord fell away; his arms parted and floated upward, the hands dimly seen on each side in the growing light. He watched them with a new interest as first one and then the other pounced upon the noose at his neck. They tore it away and thrust it fiercely aside, its undulations resembling those of a water snake. "Put it back, put it back!" He thought he shouted these words to his hands, for the undoing of the noose had been succeeded by the direst pang that he had yet experienced. His neck ached horribly; his brain was on fire; his heart, which had been fluttering faintly, gave a great leap, trying to force itself out at his mouth. His whole body was racked and wrenched with an insupportable anguish! But his disobedient hands gave no heed to the command. They beat the water vigorously with quick, downward strokes, forcing him to the surface. He felt his head emerge; his eyes were blinded by the sunlight; his chest expanded convulsively, and with a supreme and crowning agony his lungs engulfed a great draught of air, which instantly he expelled in a shriek!

He was now in full possession of his physical senses. They were, indeed, preternaturally keen and alert. Something in the awful disturbance of his organic system had so exalted and refined them that they made record of things never before perceived. He felt the ripples upon his face and heard their separate sounds as they struck. He looked at the forest on the bank of the stream, saw the individual trees, the leaves and the veining of each leaf—saw the very insects upon them: the locusts, the brilliant-bodied flies, the grey spiders stretching their webs from twig to twig. He noted the prismatic colors in all the dewdrops upon a million blades of grass. The humming of the gnats that danced above the eddies of the stream, the beating of the dragon flies' wings, the strokes of the water-spiders' legs, like oars which had lifted their boat—all these made audible music. A fish slid along beneath his eyes and he heard the rush of its body parting the water.

He had come to the surface facing down the stream; in a moment the visible world seemed to wheel slowly round, himself the pivotal point, and he saw the bridge, the fort, the soldiers upon the bridge, the captain, the sergeant, the two privates, his executioners.

They were in silhouette against the blue sky. They shouted and gesticulated, pointing at him. The captain had drawn his pistol, but did not fire; the others were unarmed. Their movements were grotesque and horrible, their forms gigantic.

Suddenly he heard a sharp report and something struck the water smartly within a few inches of his head, spattering his face with spray. He heard a second report, and saw one of the sentinels with his rifle at his shoulder, a light cloud of blue smoke rising from the muzzle. The man in the water saw the eye of the man on the bridge gazing into his own through the sights of the rifle. He observed that it was a grey eye and remembered having read that grey eyes were keenest, and that all famous marksmen had them. Nevertheless, this one had missed.

A counter swirl had caught Farquhar and turned him half round; he was again looking into the forest on the bank opposite the fort. The sound of a clear, high voice in a monotonous singsong now rang out behind him and came across the water with a distinctness that pierced and subdued all other sounds, even the beating of the ripples in his ears. Although no soldier, he had frequented camps enough to know the dread significance of that deliberate, drawling, aspirated chant; the lieutenant on shore was taking a part in the morning's work. How coldly and pitilessly–with what an even, calm intonation, presaging, and enforcing tranquillity in the men–with what accurately measured intervals fell those cruel words:

"Attention, company! . . . Shoulder arms! . . . Ready! . . . Aim! . . . Fire!"

Farquhar dived–dived as deeply as he could. The water roared in his ears like the voice of Niagara, yet he heard the dulled thunder of the volley and, rising again toward the surface, met shining bits of metal, singularly flattened, oscillating slowly downward. Some of them touched him on the face and hands, then fell away, continuing their descent. One lodged between his collar and neck; it was uncomfortably warm and he snatched it out.

As he rose to the surface, gasping for breath, he saw that he had been a long time under water; he was perceptibly farther down stream nearer to safety. The soldiers had almost finished reloading; the metal ramrods flashed all at once in the sunshine as they were drawn from the barrels, turned in the air, and thrust into their sockets. The two sentinels fired again, independently and ineffectually.

The hunted man saw all this over his shoulder; he was now swimming vigorously with the current. His brain was as energetic as his arms and legs; he thought with the rapidity of lightning.

"The officer," he reasoned, "will not make that martinet's error a second time. It is as easy to dodge a volley as a single shot. He has probably already given the command to fire at will. God help me, I cannot dodge them all!"

An appalling splash within two yards of him was followed by a loud, rushing sound, *diminuendo*, which seemed to travel back through the air to the fort and died in an explosion which stirred the very river to its deeps! A rising sheet of water curved over him, fell down upon him, blinded him, strangled him! The cannon had taken a hand in the game. As he shook his head free from the commotion of the smitten water he heard the deflected shot humming through the air ahead, and in an instant it was cracking and smashing the branches in the forest beyond.

"They will not do that again," he thought; "the next time they will use a charge of grape. I must keep my eye upon the gun; the smoke will apprise me—the report arrives too late; it lags behind the missile. That is a good gun."

Suddenly he felt himself whirled round and round—spinning like a top. The water, the banks, the forests, the now distant bridge, fort and men—all were commingled and blurred. Objects were represented by their colors only; circular horizontal streaks of color—that was all he saw. He had been caught in a vortex and was being whirled on with a velocity of advance and gyration that made him giddy and sick. In a few moments he was flung upon the gravel at the foot of the left bank of the stream—the southern bank—and behind a projecting point which concealed him from his enemies. The sudden arrest of his motion, the abrasion of one of his hands on the gravel, restored him, and he wept with delight. He dug his fingers into the sand, threw it over himself in handfuls and audibly blessed it. It looked like diamonds, rubies, emeralds; he could think of nothing beautiful which it did not resemble. The trees upon the bank were giant garden plants; he noted a definite order in their arrangement, inhaled the fragrance of their blooms. A strange, roseate light shone through the spaces among their trunks and the wind made in their branches the music of Æolian harps. He had no wish to perfect his escape—was content to remain in that enchanting spot until retaken.

A whiz and rattle of grapeshot among the branches high above his head roused him from his dream. The baffled cannoneer had fired him a random farewell. He sprang to his feet, rushed up the sloping bank, and plunged into the forest.

All that day he traveled, laying his course by the rounding sun. The forest seemed interminable; nowhere did he discover a break in it, not even a woodman's road. He had not known that he lived in so wild a region. There was something uncanny in the revelation.

By nightfall he was fatigued, footsore, famishing. The thought of his wife and children urged him on. At last he found a road which led him in what he knew to be the right direction. It was as wide and straight as a city street, yet it seemed untraveled. No fields bordered it, no dwelling anywhere. Not so much as the barking of a dog suggested human habitation. The black bodies of the trees formed a straight wall on both sides, terminating on the horizon in a point, like a diagram in a lesson in perspective. Overhead, as he looked up through this rift in the wood, shone great garden stars looking unfamiliar and grouped in strange constellations. He was sure they were arranged in some order which had a secret and malign significance. The wood on either side was full of singular noises, among which—once, twice, and again—he distinctly heard whispers in an unknown tongue.

His neck was in pain and lifting his hand to it found it horribly swollen. He knew that it had a circle of black where the rope had bruised it. His eyes felt congested; he could no longer close them. His tongue was swollen with thirst; he relieved its fever by thrusting it forward from between his teeth into the cold air. How softly the turf had carpeted the untraveled avenue—he could no longer feel the roadway beneath his feet!

Doubtless, despite his suffering, he had fallen asleep while walking, for now he sees another scene—perhaps he has merely recovered from a delirium. He stands at the gate of his own home. All is as he left it, and all bright and beautiful in the morning sunshine. He must have traveled the entire night. As he pushes open the gate and passes up the wide white walk, he sees a flutter of female garments; his wife, looking fresh and cool and sweet, steps down from the veranda to meet him. At the bottom of the steps she stands waiting, with a smile of ineffable joy, an attitude of matchless grace and dignity. Ah, how beautiful she is! He springs forward with extended arms. As he is about to clasp her he feels

a stunning blow upon the back of the neck; a blinding white light
blazes all about him with a sound like the shock of a cannon–then all
is darkness and silence!

Peyton Farquhar was dead; his body, with a broken neck,
swung gently from side to side beneath the timbers of the Owl
Creek bridge.

Commentary   Note how efficiently Bierce writes. All the
elements of a short story come together in a contained space:

- We have a **problem (or conflict)**: a main character with a
  noose around his neck. This problem works as a **trigger**,
  an event that's going to set everything in motion. (See
  Chapters 2 and 5, pages 15 and 69.)
- The problem makes for an intriguing **beginning**, with a
  natural **hook** for getting our attention. (See Chapter 5,
  page 70.)
- Bierce presents a **major dramatic question**: how's the
  main character going to get out of this mess? (See
  Chapter 2, page 18.)
- We have **stakes**: if the character doesn't come up with
  something in a minute or two, he's going to be dead. (See
  Chapter 5, page 72.)
- Bierce also gives us a **theme**: what happens to civilians
  when they try to act like soldiers? (See Chapter 1, page 7.)
- **Obstacles** and **conflicts** prevent our character from
  achieving his goal of escaping back to his home. (See
  Chapter 2, page 15.)

- There's a **point-of-view, third-person limited**, and events are described by a **reliable narrator**. (See Chapter 4, pages 51 and 52.)
- We have some Union **antagonists** to go with our Confederate **protagonist**. (See Chapter 3, page 26.)
- We have **settings** and **characters** described with precise, specific **details**. (See Chapter 6, pages 102–104.)
- There's **dialogue**, but not too much; this story doesn't have much space for it. (See Chapter 7.)
- Bierce writes a dramatic **climax**—things don't turn out so well for the civilian-turned-saboteur—that's so powerful we don't need a **dénouement**. (See Chapter 5, pages 84 and 85.)
- The story has a memorable **twist ending** that turns the whole story on its head. (See Chapter 5, page 90.)

Also remarkable is how Bierce trimmed the fat from his text. Everything here has a purpose. Despite its small size—the story is only 3,700 words—"An Occurrence at Owl Creek Bridge" manages to take us on a long and eventful journey.

A Final Note

Learning to write an excellent short story is an ongoing process. Every story you write will be different—each will have a different plot, different characters, and a different structure. Each time you sit down and begin developing your story or writing a first draft, you'll have to start from the very beginning. However, understanding the basic elements of a short story will help take the mystery out of writing. No matter what kind of story you're working on, you'll know exactly what to do, every step of the way.

Like anything else, practice makes perfect. As you write, you'll discover your own writing style and your own best strategies for creating a compelling, memorable story. You'll work out the kinks and see how all the parts work together to help you write an excellent story, every time.

Don't let that blank page or computer screen scare you off! Now you know what to do, so you can get started. Good luck!

About the Authors

John Vorwald is a freelance writer. He lives in New York City.

Ethan Wolff is a freelance writer and editor in New York City.